Osprey Classic Library

Osprey Classic Library

Triumph Spitfire and GT6

**Spitfire 1, 2, 3, IV, 1500;
GT6 1, 2, 3**

Graham Robson

Published in 1982 by Osprey Publishing Ltd
12–14 Long Acre, London WC2E 9LP
Member company of the George Philip Group

British Library Cataloguing in Publication Data
Robson, Graham
  Triumph-Spitfire. — (Osprey classic library)
  I. Triumph Spitfire automobile — History
  I. Title
  629.2′222   TL215.T7

ISBN 0-85045-452-2

Editor: Tim Parker
Design: Norman Brownsword

Filmset and printed by BAS Printers Limited
Over Wallop, Hampshire

Contents

Introduction

I have always believed that the Triumph Spitfire was a very under-rated car. Not only did it always look nicer than its rivals, but it was invariably faster. In addition—and this, surely, is the clincher—it outsold them as well. Now that the last Spitfire has been produced, this book is a wide-ranging attempt to set the record straight.

Perhaps it was always inevitable that I would eventually write a book about Spitfires and GT6s, for they have always been rather dear to me. Not only was I one of the very first motoring enthusiasts to set eyes on a Spitfire, but I was also privileged to be closely involved in the competitions development of the design. Even while I was first seeing the Spitfire, and being captivated by its styling, I was an Austin-Healey Sprite owner. It has to be an ideal qualification.

I may have fallen in love with the Spitfire on the day I first saw the prototype. The date was May 1961, I was just beginning a new job in the experimental department of Standard-Triumph, and I was being shown around the workshops. Right away, I was smitten by the car's looks, an impression later intensified when I began driving the proto-types, and the early production models.

Later, too, I recall seeing the fastback Spitfire GT when Michelotti had just finished it, driving that car (converted to six cylinder power) in France, and seeing the GT6 evolve from it. Even after I moved on from Standard-Triumph, in 1965, I kept my links with the department, for I always had a personal interest in these cars.

Was I always too close to the Spitfire to take a balanced view of its merits? I don't think so. I followed up ownership of the Sprite with one of the first Mk 1 Spitfires, and immediately reconfirmed all the advantages of the little Triumph. In any case, it wasn't only my own opinion which counted. To put it bluntly, '314,000 customers can't be wrong'.

The last Triumph Spitfire of all was built in the summer of 1980, but it was a car which had died slowly, of neglect. Like several other sports cars in that in January 1975 the ill-fated TR7 was profitable, company, the Spitfire would have been updated in 1974. It may be no coincidence that in the autumn of that year, major changes were made to the Spitfire, the MG Midget, and the MGB, and that in January 1975 the ill-fated TR7 was launched. Nor can it be purely by chance that the effective nationalization of the corporation took place shortly afterwards. In a well-managed, and profitable, company, the Spitfire would have been re-designed, or replaced, years earlier.

With the benefit of hindsight, therefore, I have tried to relate the life story of the Spitfire—of the car itself, of the people who influenced its career, and of the models spawned from it. Because I have always realized that it was sales in North America which governed the viability of the project, I have also given special attention to that market, and I want to make it quite clear that it was my distinguished North American friend and colleague, Richard Langworth, who provided Chapters 8 and 10, and who advised me on so many other aspects of the car.

Have I provided too many facts, figures, and statistics? Perhaps I have—but they all help to flesh out the life and times of a great car. A great car? Why not. It lived for 18 years, and made a multitude of friends. When more mundane Triumph, and British Leyland, products are gone and forgotten, the Spitfire will live on. With a name like that, how could it fail?

Acknowledgements

In many ways, this book took 20 years to write, and there must be hundreds of kind people who have helped me, directly or indirectly, to assemble the Spitfire story. To use the time-honoured cliché, they are far too numerous to list.

I'd better start, therefore, by thanking Richard Langworth, my personal North American connection, not only for providing research assistance, and for personally providing Chapters 8 and 10, but also for being a fount of historical wisdom and common sense. Richard is that rather rare breed among Americans—he is not only an Anglophile to end all Anglophiles, but actually knows all about his subject. Richard told me things about the Spitfire I should have known, but didn't. Is it likely that I can ever tell him anything about an American car? I doubt it.

Next, because without him there would never have been a Spitfire, and because he has always answered my questions—sensible or asinine—I salute Harry Webster. At the time that he was designing the Spitfire, Harry looked on it as no more than another job to be faithfully and competently done; later he came to realize what a special little car it actually was. Even when he was frantically busy at British Leyland in the early 1970s, or exploring the frontiers of transmission technology with Automotive Products later in that decade, he always found time to make sure my facts were right, and my opinions at least supportable.

Nor would I ever have got the full story without consulting John Lloyd from time to time. John, who managed the experimental workshops when the Spitfire was being conceived, was always Harry Webster's right-hand-man, and eventually became technical director of Rover-Triumph in his own right, was the humorist who could always defuse any tense situation, or the man who could draw on vast reserves of engineering experience to solve any knotty little problem. John Lloyd it was who led the Herald expedition across the Sahara in 1958, and master-minded the Spitfire Le Mans assaults of 1964 and 1965; he seemed to enjoy doing both, and he certainly did them superbly.

Over the years I have reminisced with important personalities such as John Carpenter, Lyndon Mills, Ray Henderson, and Fred Nicklin. Legions of Standard-Triumph and British Leyland PR staff have toiled to put me in touch with the right statisticians, and make the correct records available to me. At one point, incidentally, I was privileged to study confidential director's records that only one other author has ever been shown, and I am grateful for that. Latterly, too, it was Peter Carpenter, Patrick Jeal, and Bert Elmer of the Engineering Division, who guided me so kindly through the complexities of North American specifications for Spitfire and GT6 models.

The book, of course, would have been valueless without a huge selection of pictures, and here I must thank Norman James of the Triumph Photographic Department for all his help. Not only did he let me spend many hours delving into the archive books, the catalogues, and the negative stores, but he also printed a mass of 'new' pictures to tell a complicated story. For this reason, I think I can claim that most of the illustrations used have not been seen in public before. Other photographs came from F. Wilson McComb, Lotus Cars and John Brandwood.

Which brings me to another North American connection—Mike Cook, of BL's North American subsidiary in New Jersey—who has known me, humoured me, and helped me, on and off, for nearly 20 years. Richard Langworth and I both know that without him, the 'Spitfire story' in North America might have been lost in the mists of time.

I ought to sign off, however, with a posthumous tribute—to the genius of Giovanni Michelotti. No one, especially Alick Dick and Harry Webster, seriously believes that the Spitfire could ever have been a success if it had not had such sensational and instantly recognizable styling. Without the little Italian, there could have been no Spitfire; indeed, without him, there could have been no successful 1960's Triumphs at all. When Standard-Triumph merged into British Leyland at the end of the 1960s, Michelotti's influence began to fade. It shows—in the new models which arrived much later, and in the lack of sparkle they exhibited. Michelotti died at the end of the 1970s, well before his true genius was recognized. This book, perhaps, will do something to rectify that.

Graham Robson
Burton Bradstock, Dorset
January 1982

7

Chapter 1
Origins: an Italian and the Herald

Direct development of a new small Triumph sports car—code-named *Bomb* at the time, and soon to be known as Spitfire—began in 1960, but its true origins are to be found much earlier. However, to get back to the real start of a story with any precision can be as difficult as tracing the authentic source of a great river like the Amazon. In the case of the Spitfire, however, I think I must start with the birth of a new engine—the SC (Small Car) unit, in 1951.

The Triumph company name had been acquired by the Standard Motor Company in 1944. From 1923 to 1939 Triumph cars had been made by an independent Coventry concern (which had been in the motorcycle manufacturing business since 1902, but which had hived off the two-wheeler side of things in 1936). Money troubles in the 1930s led to bankruptcy in 1939, after which Triumph's assets were taken over by Thos. W. Ward Ltd, of Sheffield. During the war this company indulged in a little judicious asset-stripping, before selling off the remains to Standard, whose managing director was the redoubtable and dynamic Sir John Black.

In recent times Sir John had enjoyed a turbulent relationship with William Lyons, who built SS-Jaguars, and we now know that his first thoughts were to develop new sporting Standard-based Triumphs with which to do battle with Lyons and his cars (and, if the truth be told, to massage his own ego as a visionary tycoon). It was not until 1953, however, when the legendary TR2 sports car was put on sale, that he appeared to have aimed straight. By this time, in any case, his target had shifted—for Jaguar were right out of the S-T league—and henceforth he was to concentrate on hitting out at MG and Austin-Healey, both marques produced by the British Motor Corporation.

In the meantime, all-new Standard economy saloons had been developed, and were selling fairly well; these utilized promising new engines and transmissions. The first postwar Standards had been re-worked Flying Standard Eights of 1938-9 vintage, and the next small saloons had been badged as Triumph Mayflowers, saddled with controversial razor-edge body styles, and powered by further derivations of that 1930s side-valve Standard engine.

The first truly postwar small Standard to be new from end to end, however, was the SC project, which began to take shape in 1951, and it was here that the Spitfire had its original roots. In the beginning, this car was to have been rear-engined, might have used some of the Mayflower's suspension, and could even have used the same side-valve engine with a non-synchromesh three-speed gearbox. By the end of 1951, however, it was decided that SC should have an all-new pushrod overhead valve engine, and a four-speed gearbox with central change (and synchromesh on top, third and second gears), together with a new light-duty hypoid back axle, all under a new unit-construction bodyshell. That shell, incidentally, was to be built for Standard by Fisher & Ludlow—an independent body-building concern when SC was being planned, but taken over by BMC in 1953 just as production got under way.

The engine, gearbox, and final drive had cost a fortune in investment capital, and were obviously

---

ABOVE RIGHT: *The first 'Standard' Triumph—the 1800 Roadster of 1946 1949*

RIGHT: *The Spitfire story really started with this car—the Standard Eight of 1953, which had an all new four-cylinder 803 cc engine, and four-speed gearbox. It was this engine/gearbox combination which was developed for the Herald, then for the Spitfire in the 1960s*

destined for many years' use, even if SC—now publicly known as the Standard Eight—was not. Standard-Triumph's critical problem, when considering a successor to the SC range, was not to design new engines, but to find anyone prepared to build bodyshells for them. Alick Dick, who had become Standard-Triumph's managing director in 1954 after the increasingly-mercurial Sir John Black had been ousted, remembers this as the major event which affected the company's forward planning in the late 1950s, 'I went over to see Leonard Lord,' (Lord was chairman of BMC, who now owned Fisher & Ludlow), 'to see if they would make the bodies. He said, "How many do you want?", and I said, "2000 a week", at which he then retorted, "I'm not going to use the company's capital for the benefit of the Standard Motor Company"'.

It was at this time that the idea of reverting to the use of a separate chassis frame for the new model began to take shape, though the one development was not exactly the result of the other event. For

some time, Alick Dick, Martin Tustin (the company's general manager since 1955), and Harry Webster (chief designer under Ted Grinham at the time, and chief engineer from 1957) had been looking for a new product which would be relatively cheap to tool-up, and which could easily be assembled at Standard-Triumph's other factories in India, Australia, South Africa, and perhaps in new locations in underdeveloped countries. They wanted a car which could be built in different body styles—saloon, coupé, estate car, convertible, and van—without disturbing the general engineering layout of the design.

In the meantime, Alick Dick was still casting around for an alternative supply of bodyshells in

When Triumph decided on a separate chassis for their Herald, they even tried a multi-tube frame like this. It wasn't strong enough, or cheap enough

Britain. After Fisher & Ludlow, the only viable alternative for a monocoque shell was the Pressed Steel Co. (of Cowley, Oxford). But apart from the fact that they were already flooded out with tooling work for regular customers, and could not do Standard-Triumph's job in time, Dick was worried about their industrial status, 'I began to think on the lines of Once bitten, Twice shy, and thought that if someone took over Pressed Steel we could be in the same position again. There's no doubt that that talk with Len Lord coloured my whole outlook. . . .'

Standard-Triumph, therefore, were virtually forced to the conclusion that they should plan on building their own bodies—initially by buying a company, or companies, to do the job for them, and eventually by developing their own expertise. They had already signed an agreement with Mulliners of Birmingham in 1954, whereby that company would build up its supplies to Standard-Triumph, and eventually wind down all other existing contracts; Mulliners took over another concern, Forward Radiator, in 1957, and were themselves acquired by Standard-Triumph in 1958. However, even though Mulliners were supplying complete TR3 sports car bodies, along with estate car and van derivatives of the Standard Vanguard and Standard 10hp models, they were not large enough to tackle tooling and manufacture of a completely new mass-production saloon bodyshell.

It was with all this in mind, therefore, that Alick Dick set about acquiring its body stamping capability in stages—which included the purchase of Hall Engineering (Holdings) in Liverpool, and a tooling company known as Auto Body Dies of Dunstable.

In the meantime, Harry Webster and Martin Tustin had decided not only that they *had* to revert

The sports car which started the TR revolution—the first TR2 of 1953, with Ken Richardson at the wheel

BELOW: *The SC engine/gearbox assembly as refined for the Herald of 1959. The gearbox was the Herald's four-speed which, in almost exactly this form, was to be used in every Spitfire built between 1962 and 1970. It had no synchromesh on first gear at first*

RIGHT: *Cutaway anatomy of the 1959 Herald Coupé, showing the separate chassis, and the independent front and rear suspensions. All were vitally important to the birth of the Spitfire*

ABOVE: *The style which started a revolution at Triumph — that of the Herald Coupe. The directors were so delighted by this car when they first saw it on Christmas Eve 1957 that they immediately went out and started the celebrations!*

RIGHT: *A familiar layout to Spitfire owners? This, in fact, is a Herald saloon, though in all major respects the layout is the same*

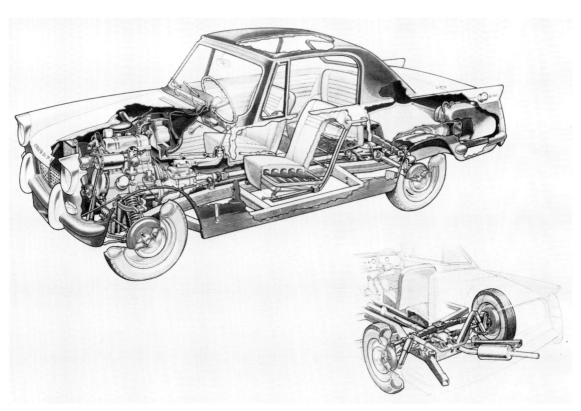

LEFT: *This display version of the Herald shows that the Coupé was a definite, if rather uncomfortable, four-seater. The Spitfire could have a considerably shortened wheelbase, and still provide a spacious two-seater layout*

BELOW: *The Herald Coupé was an active works competition car, always let down by its high weight and comparative lack of power. This was Cyril Corbishley's car in the 1960 Monte Carlo Rally*

BELOW LEFT: *The first drop-head version of this basic design was the Herald Convertible—this being a 1960 model, shown with the roof partly furled*

LEFT: *The very first 'egg-box' wooden mock-up of the new Bomb sports car, at the Michelotti workshops in 1960. Note that there is a bulge in the proposed bonnet panel, not used on the car which was built*

BELOW LEFT: *The* Bomb *mock-up, summer 1960, with the door-top line already altered to suit Harry Webster's need to touch the ground when trailing his arm over the side*

BELOW: *Building the first production-standard Spitfire prototype in March 1962. The chassis looks right, but the drum brakes and single carburettor engine are only there to prove the layout of the frame itself. Neither was used on the road cars*

to a separate chassis frame for the new car, code-named *Zobo*, but that they actively *wanted* to do so. As Harry Webster once told me, 'We had to provide a good foundation for assembling all those different bits and pieces,' (different versions of the same body design), 'and if we sent "knocked-down" cars for assembly to other countries, we could use the chassis as a jig if necessary.'

It all seemed to make a lot of sense, particularly as the rather piece-meal method of acquiring body-making capacity also led to the brave decision to have the body supplied in sections, for bolt-up assembly (rather than weld-up assembly) in Co-ventry. To round it all off, Len Lord's refusal to supply Standard-Triumph with bodyshells from the Fisher & Ludlow factory at Tile Hill, Coventry, meant that that factory was now redundant to his needs—whereupon Standard-Triumph put in an offer to buy it, and were accepted!

ABOVE: *Three-quarter rear view of the* Bomb *prototype of 1960—for the production car the only major exterior modification would be to fit new quarter bumpers, and to raise the line of the door tops very slightly. In all other respects, however, Michelotti's first effort was the right one*

ABOVE LEFT: *The* Bomb *prototype, just arrived at Coventry from Turin in October 1960, with no hood mechanism, but otherwise looking very like the final product*

LEFT: *Somehow, Michelotti's fascia styles were never as nice as his overall body lines. This was the original* Bomb *of October 1960, using all the instruments and controls from the Herald Coupé which had been 'cannibalised' in its construction. All in all, the interior was too stark*

All this, however, took time, especially as it was taking an age to arrive at acceptable body styles. The story of how the young Italian stylist, Giovanni Michelotti, was introduced to Standard-Triumph by businessman Captain Raymond Flower has often been told. It was after Flower's claim that he knew an Italian who could not only style, but have built, prototype bodies in two to three months, that

Michelotti was taken under contract to Standard-Triumph. His first job was to produce the be-finned TR3-based 'dream car' of 1957, his next was to re-touch the Series III Vanguard into the Vignale Vanguard, and his third was to apply his genius to the *Zobo* project. His distinctive *Zobo* style was completed in the summer of 1957, and the first prototype bodyshell (the original Herald Coupé) arrived in Coventry on Christmas Eve 1957. After which, as Harry Webster told me: 'We put it straight into the styling studio, on the turntable, and we were all so thrilled with that coupé body style that we all downed tools and went out for a pint!'

Cost targets for the new car, which had been named Herald after Alick Dick's own boat, were very tight, and this partly explains why the very versatile independent front suspension was matched by a rather cheap and nasty swing-axle independent rear suspension. Harry Webster has since stated that his engineers always wanted to use the pivoting-spring type of swing axle layout which was not adopted on the Spitfire until the start up of Mk IV production, but that cost limits killed it off for many years. Besides, he insists, the suspension was perfectly adequate for its original purpose, which did not include the development of a sports car from the basic layout.

The Triumph Herald, therefore, went into production at the beginning of 1959, was announced in April 1959, and caused quite a stir in the technical press. Not only, on the one hand, had it effectively stepped back a decade in constructional terms (most of Britain's 'Big Six' manufacturers made the move to unit-construction bodyshells by the end of the 1940s, and here was one of them reversing the trend), but it broke considerable new ground in terms of section-by-section body construction. It offered different body styles using this principle and all-independent suspension. In addition, prototypes had completed a very publicity-worthy proving trip from Cape Town, in South Africa, to Tangier, in Morocco, captured so vividly in a series of *Motor* features written by Richard Bensted-Smith, and succinctly titled *Turn Left for Tangier*.

The main 'building blocks'—the cars, the engineering policies, and the commercial deals which affected everything—to influence the birth of the Spitfire were all in place by the end of the 1950s. By this time, Alick Dick had sold out Standard-Triumph's interests in the Ferguson tractor operation, had spent most of the money accruing from that deal in buying a variety of components firms, and had committed more to the building of a huge

The original Triumph-built Spitfire prototype of 1962, still without its bumpers, but otherwise to production standards. This car was eventually registered 412VC, and the backdrop is rural Warwickshire

new assembly hall at Canley (Coventry), and to the expansion of body pressing and assembly facilities at Speke, near Liverpool. The fact that the Herald's doubtful quality reputation was already becoming known was only one of the clouds on the horizon, and the first signs of an 'overheating' British economy was another.

In 1959, however, the Standard-Triumph board of directors were in a happy and confident mood. They foresaw independence from most outside suppliers by the early 1960s, and their sales force were forecasting sales of nearly 185,000 for the financial year 1960–61. Profits for 1958–9 had been £2.2 millions after tax, and everything looked set fair.

In the meantime, Triumph's sports car sales were booming all around the world, not least in North America, as the TR3A's reputation reached its peak. TR3A sales might not quite have reached those of the MGA from Abingdon (in 1959, to be exact, Triumph produced 21,298 TR3As, while total MGA production of all types, including the Twin-Cam, was 23,319 cars), but they were quite phenomenal by any previous Triumph standards. A new range of TRs— coded as *Zoom* and *Zest*— was already being planned, with production due to begin in 1961.

At the MG factory at Abingdon, another very successful sports car was making its name. In 1958, the combination of Donald Healey's design ability, and the 'can-do' abilities of MG planners, had given birth to the cheap, cheerful, and very promising Austin-Healey Sprite. In its own way, the little 'Frog Eye' was setting all sorts of trends—it combined an existing power train and 'chassis' in a new body/chassis structure, to offer remarkable value for money at the bottom end of the market. In 1958, when the A35-engined Sprite was revealed, its British basic price was £445, which compared very favourably with the £663 asked for the MGA, and the £699 asked for the Triumph TR3A.

In its own way, the Sprite did exactly what Triumph were tempted to do for themselves, but Triumph were certainly capable of doing a more professional job. The Sprite, in fact, looked quite ugly (or 'cute', if you were an Abingdon/Healey devotee, and never admitted to the cars having any failings), it had a very cramped interior, along with

Everything open on the Triumph-built prototype. Only the different fascia style gives the game away

a crude rear suspension. Even with all those obvious handicaps, more than 21,000 Sprites were built in its first full calendar year, 1959.

The Sprite succeeded, in spite of its specification, because it was first. At the time, no other car built anywhere in the world could offer sports car enthusiasts such a value-for-money combination of performance, mechanical simplicity, ease of maintenance, and price; the Italians, Alfa Romeo and Fiat, were far too busy looking up market to bother themselves with this bargain basement. Indeed, it is fair to say that BMC, by launching the Austin-Healey Sprite, created a new market.

Although the arrival of the Sprite was not the only factor which encouraged Standard-Triumph to design a small-engined sports car of their own, it

was an important influence on them. John Carpenter, who was then Standard's general sales manager, recalled the feeling that, 'the idea of building a small sports car started with Harry Webster. Going right back, I'm sure we all developed the feeling that the TR now needed a smaller vehicle alongside it. It seemed to some of us that there was a niche for a smaller, inexpensive little car at a price above the Sprite but below the level of MGA and TR, and of course it was the American market that we were going to rely on. America was the platform on which all sports car volume was based.'

Harry Webster confirms this, 'We were already looking for ways of using the Herald's chassis engineering, and a sports car was obviously on the cards after the success of the TR range.' At the time, there was no such thing as formal product planning at Standard-Triumph; Webster told me that, 'George Turnbull, as manufacturing director, was always close to Alick Dick, and we used to sort things out for ourselves—Alick, George and I—before the board of directors was asked to formalize anything.

April 1962—the fascia style originally proposed for the Spitfire, without a rev-counter and still using Herald Coupé instruments. Fortunately it was dropped after a very short time

I think you could say that the Spitfire project started between three of us—George Turnbull, Michelotti, the stylist, and myself.'

John Lloyd, who ran the experimental and development workshops, thinks that Harry Webster is being rather too modest, reminding me that Harry used to make regular trips to and from the Italian stylist's studios in Turin, usually by road, often as frequently as once a fortnight. The Spitfire, I am assured, must surely have taken shape as a result of the regular contact between Webster and Michelotti.

Early in 1960, however, by which time the Sprite had been in production for nearly two years, a small Triumph sports car project got under way. Webster had settled on the wheelbase of 83 in.—8.5 in. shorter than that of the four-seater Herald, and an important three inches longer than that of the Sprite—had decided that the new car should use as much existing Herald hardware as possible, and set Michelotti to work. A complete 948 cc Herald car was driven out to Turin, where the body was swiftly discarded, the chassis carved about, and construction of a prototype began.

'As usual we had asked Michelotti to submit a selection of drawings, just styling sketches really,' Harry Webster told me. 'He supplied five or six, done in the space of no more than four or five days (sometimes I've known him to do ten, at least—he worked tremendously quickly), George and I chose the style we liked, and sent him off to do the full-size drawings, and to build the wooden body buck.'

Right from the start, Webster, in conjunction with Arthur Ballard, his chief body design engineer, had decided that the bodyshell of the new car, now code-named *Bomb* by his whimsical administrators, should have a rigid welded-up scuttle, floor and tail section, and that the entire bonnet/front wings/

Fred Nicklin, one of Triumph's test and development drivers, who had much to do with the refinement of the original Spitfire. Here he sits in a Herald Convertible

wheel arch section should be pivoted from the front of the chassis, just as it was in the Herald design. The major difference was that the Herald chassis was not merely to be shortened, but that the entire layout of the frame was to be modified. Front and rear suspensions, and the general disposition of the power train, was to be the same as the Herald, but the chassis frame strength was to be centred in the main backbone box-section members. Unlike the Herald, there were to be no chassis side members, but great strength was to be built into the bodyshell by providing it with box sections doubling up as sills.

Left to Right, Harry Webster, Giovanni Michelotti and Martin Tustin, the team who were involved with the birth of the Spitfire in 1960 and 1961

For the sake of historical accuracy, however, I should make it clear that the very first frame used, under the prototype built in Turin, was merely a cut-and-shut Herald frame, with the side members removed and the outriggers modified. The definitive frame, although following roughly the same lines, was to be more rigid, and entirely different in detail.

Confidential boardroom documents first mention the 'Herald Sports Car project' in April 1960, which is fair enough, as the Herald had been in quantity production since the early spring of 1959. At this time, by the way, its body construction was not settled, for both steel and fibreglass were being discussed. By September 1960, the directors were ready to authorize the construction of a mock-up of the *Bomb*, but this minute was really a case of closing the stable door after the horse had bolted, for the

Webster/Turnbull team had approved a start on the prototype some weeks earlier, and the complete and running prototype actually arrived in Coventry towards the end of October! As far as Michelotti was concerned, once the broad lines had been agreed, his tiny workshop (with only four multiskilled craftsmen) could get on with building a car.

Although the car which arrived in Coventry looked very much like that eventually put on sale in the autumn of 1962, it was not the style which had been approved at sketch stage nor, indeed, the car which Michelotti had started building earlier in 1960.

'One outstanding memory I have of the wooden buck—it looked rather like an eggbox in some ways, but it was built so that you could sit in it even though the doors didn't open—is that at first it didn't have a dip in its waistline. I hated it, I really did, and I told

Michelotti that I wanted it to look a bit more traditional. So he put a little dip in it, then a bit more, but it still wasn't right. In the end, I sat in it, on a makeshift seat absolutely in the right position, dropped my arm over the side, and told him "I want my fingers to be able to brush the floor". He altered the door top to make that possible, and I reckon it looked a lot better.'

Getting the prototype back to the factory in Coventry was simple enough, but getting it into production was not. By the autumn of 1960

Alick Dick (standing) and Sir John Black, the two chief executives of Standard-Triumph in the 1940s and 1950s. It was Alick Dick's enthusiasm which led to the birth of the Spitfire

Standard-Triumph's finances were in disarray, and the company was losing a lot of money. As Alick Dick once said 'Money was pouring out like water. It was absolutely terrifying.' A collapse of the British car market, a rapid contraction in exports to North America, and over-production of the TR3A were all to blame. Without an approach from a larger concern, Standard-Triumph might have folded within six months.

The winter of 1960-61 was a traumatic period for Standard-Triumph, and their entire corporate future was affected. At the time, no one knew if existing models would survive, or if any new models would ever appear. For a time, the *Bomb* project looked to be doomed. Like the happy ending which winds up every fairy tale, however, a financial saviour appeared. Just when it began to look as if Standard-Triumph must close down, they received a formal approach from Leyland Motors. To Alick Dick, it must have looked as if all his troubles were over. If only he had known, they were just about to begin.

BELOW LEFT: *Alick Dick (right) and Giovanni Michelotti at the launch of the Herald in 1959. They had much to be proud of*

BELOW: *Harry Webster, without whose vision the Herald and Spitfire cars might never have been built. In this picture he is looking at Triumph 1300 schemes and modifications*

Chapter 2
Mergers: Triumph and Leyland

If only the *Bomb* project had been started a couple of years earlier, the subsequent history of the British motor industry might have been radically changed. If only Standard-Triumph had pushed ahead with this striking little sports car instead of dabbling with non-starters like the *Atlas* van and the *Zero* tractor, their corporate fortunes might have been entirely different. If only. . . .

The problem facing Standard-Triumph was that they were too small. Ever since he had become the company's managing director in 1954, at the remarkably young age of 37, Alick Dick had realized this, and had been searching for a corporate partner. Even with the help of healthy profits brought in by the making of Ferguson tractors, he was convinced that his company could not face the future alone. In Britain, at the time, several other car-making concerns were similarly placed, and Dick became determined to merge Standard-Triumph with one of them.

His failure to do so was one reason why Standard-Triumph came to face a monumental cash crisis in the winter of 1960–61. His 1959 decision to simplify things by taking the company out of an existing 12-year tractor production agreement with Massey-Ferguson (in exchange for a large cash payment), was another. Standard-Triumph's heavy capital spending programme, not only on major new models like the Herald, but on the purchase of foundries, pressings facilities, and suspensions experts to make them more self-sufficient, was ill-timed.

In retrospect, Alick Dick, and his fellow directors at Standard-Triumph, were desperately unlucky, for if their expansion programme had been completed while the British economy was still buoyant, and the American market still snapping up European sports cars, things might have been very different. In 1959, even in the spring of 1960, the

Bomb sports car project was an attractive little indulgence which the directors were happy to approve; in the autumn of 1960 it suddenly looked like becoming a beautiful, but unwanted, orphan.

On its own, there was no doubt that *Bomb* was a very promising machine. Unfortunately, with the company so rapidly slipping towards bankruptcy, it could not be considered on its own. The Herald was already building a reputation for poor quality in spite of its enterprising specification. The TR3A was beginning to look long in the tooth, and stocks were too high. The Pennant looked awful and was struggling. The Vanguard, even with a six-cylinder engine about to be transplanted into it, was virtually unsaleable. In spite of the fact that 1959–60 profits had been reported at £1.8 million after tax, all the pointers were gloomy.

It wasn't only *Bomb* which looked like being cancelled. A proposal to re-tool the Herald body for production at Pressed Steel Co. was dropped, the *Zebu* (Vanguard-replacement) project was axed, and the idea of building TRS twin-cam *Sabrina* engines was side-lined for the moment. Before the end of 1960 the company was losing £600,000 every month.

The story of the rescue bid from Leyland Motors, the much-respected truck and bus manufacturing concern from Lancashire, has been told many times before. Harry Webster remembers clearly that Alick Dick first mentioned the existence of secret talks with Leyland at the beginning of 1960 (at a time when Standard-Triumph's affairs were still buoyant), and other sources confirm that formal discussions began in October. The proposed merger was reported officially to the Standard-Triumph board on 5 December 1960, and became public on the same day.

Leyland Motors directors took control at once, with Sir Henry Spurrier becoming chairman, and with (among others) Stanley Markland and Donald Stokes joining the board. By this time Martin Tustin had already moved out, to become the President of Standard-Triumph Inc., in North America. Right from the start, it became clear that Standard-Triumph's finances were in a parlous state (the bank overdraft was more than £9 millions in April 1961), and that drastic action was needed.

Even though the revised, and improved, Herald 1200 was announced in April 1961, and soon won many orders, it was not enough to do the trick. The Vanguard Six was still failing, and the TR4 was still not yet ready for launch.

The crunch came on 17 August when Sir Henry Spurrier and Stanley Markland (who was already, incidentally, managing director of Albion Motors, and Sir Henry's deputy at Leyland) visited Coventry. In a decisive, and (in business terms) brutal operation, they sacked almost the entire board of Standard-Triumph directors, including Alick Dick, who left the company that very day. Markland was

installed as managing director, with Donald Stokes in charge of sales, and effectively operating as his right-hand man.

While all this corporate maneouvring was going on, *Bomb* had been sitting, unwanted, under a dust sheet in the corner of the experimental workshops. The author, who joined the department as a humble development engineer in the spring of 1961, remembers that dust sheet very well. It was one of several interesting new-model projects held up by the business upheaval.

Leyland's immediate action on taking control of Standard-Triumph was to cut down on expenditure, especially on new product development.

Stanley Markland (left, accepting The Motor's *trophy commemorating a 'Best British' performance in the 1961 Le Mans race) who was charged with the difficult job of returning Standard-Triumph to profitability in 1961*

History records that 800 members of the staff were dismissed, and it also records that sales were running at well under 6000 cars a month—less than half those promised Alick Dick by his expansionary sales division in the autumn of 1959.

Harry Webster has told me on several occasions (and I can confirm this by my own observations) that Stanley Markland took a close interest in the new-model proposals as soon as he became a director. On several occasions, the dour Lancashire man was taken on a guided tour of the design offices and the workshops, probing here, asking a question there, and occasionally taking a drive in one of the prototypes.

'One day,' Harry Webster recalls, 'we were walking round the shops, and at one point we quite literally came to a halt in front of the hump under a dust sheet. "What's that", Stanley wanted to know, and when I whipped off the sheet to show him the *Bomb* he instantly said, "That's nice, what's it all about, and how far has it got?".'

'I told him that this was the single running prototype, that it was really more of a quick lash-up than the final design, that it had been assessed, but that it had been shelved for lack of funds.

'I shall never forget what happened next. He looked at it, he sat in it, he walked round it, then he turned to me and said, "That's good. We'll make that". He never even referred back to Sir Henry Spurrier, or to Donald Stokes—he approved it personally, there and then.'

A check back into company records confirms this. The management upheaval came on 17 August 1961, but approval of tooling expenditure for the *Bomb* project was given at a board meeting on 13 July. No launch date was mentioned, but it was tacitly assumed that the car would be revealed at the 1962 Earls Court Motor Show.

In preparing this book, I have been lucky to find pictures taken at the factory on 31 October 1960, showing the state of the *Bomb* prototype as received from Turin earlier that week: The car as shown in these historic pictures was not changed at all in the next nine months—indeed, John Lloyd recalls that it spent most of that time under the dust sheet, in suspended animation.

The decision was taken that the bodyshell should be manufactured at the Forward Radiator works in Bordesley Green, near the centre of Birmingham. At this point, therefore, it should be noted that Mulliners of Birmingham already had a 51 per cent holding in the Forward Radiator Co. when they themselves were absorbed by Standard-Triumph in 1958, and that they took complete control in January 1960. Until the summer of 1961 the TR3A had been built at the Mulliners' factory, but the tooling was then moved to the Forward Radiator factory for the final batch of look-alike TR3Bs to be assembled. When TR3B body production ended, in the summer of 1962, Forward Radiator was to be re-jigged for *Bomb* production to begin. The figure of £200,000 for body tooling was ludicrously low, even by early-1960s standards, and it is a fact that some of the tooling was of a very temporary 'knife-and-fork' quality at first. (Once it was realized how successful the Spitfire was going to be, however, more costly and more permanent tooling and assembly jigging was speedily laid down.)

Once *Bomb* was officially reborn—and the development was as decisive as this, for no clandestine work had been carried out while the new-model investment freeze was in operation—it was time for the important 'productionizing' process to begin. I have already made clear that the Michelotti prototype had been built up around a cut-and-shut Herald chassis with the outer side-members removed, but much more was involved than merely drawing up the body style as finalized by Michelotti and Harry Webster, and adapting it to a definitive backbone frame.

A study of the illustrations of the prototype show that its lines were virtually unaltered before being committed for production. Two important changes, however, were to the facia style, and to the doors. The prototype had been equipped with doors having no windows, side curtains, nor the means of working them, neither was there a hood of any type. Michelotti's fascia had been made up in a hurry, using the instruments from the Herald Coupé whose body had been discarded before shortening the chassis, along with the knobs and switches, and was a very basic, metal-painted, affair.

For the production car, therefore, the top line of the doors was raised very slightly, and glass wind-down windows were installed. It had always been intended that a production version of *Bomb* should be so equipped. Standard-Triumph had already decided to abandon the crudities of sliding side-screens when the TR3A was replaced, for the TR4 had wind-down windows, and it entered production in the autumn of 1961; as far as the Michelotti prototype was concerned, there had neither been time, nor the necessity, of installing winding windows. Until the spring of 1964, therefore,

Standard-Triumph had an obvious, and very significant, marketing advantage over the Sprite/Midget, which still had sliding screens.

For the hood, the designers settled for a very simple tubular linkage. When stowed, this was carried in clips around the top of the fuel tank, with access from the boot; when erect, the ends of the hoop merely slotted into tubes welded to the sides of the bodyshell, immediately behind the door shut face. No detachable hardtop was available at first though (with the successful experience of the TR2/3/3A/4 models behind them) the designers already had one planned. There was no need to change Michelotti's windscreen style, for it was exactly the same as that already put into production for the

The fascia style (like so many proposed by Michelotti from time to time) was not liked by the engineers and directors, so a new one was designed. This placed the instruments in a central

panel, and allowed the conversion from left-hand to right-hand drive to be simple and cost-effective.

Even before a representative example of the new design could be built, it was decided to find out exactly what the Michelotti-Webster-Turnbull triumvirate had produced. The original prototype, still fitted with its 52 bhp (gross) Herald Coupé 948 cc engine, was taken to MIRA for performance tests, where it recorded a maximum speed of 88.7 mph, with 0–60 mph acceleration of 16.8 sec. So far, so good. Even at that point it was faster than the newly-launched MG Midget—considerably

Donald Stokes (left) and George Turnbull making a tour of the Herald/Spitfire production line in the early 1960s. Stokes later became Sir Donald, then Lord Stokes, as he made the Leyland group bigger and ever bigger

faster—and that was before the lustier 1147 cc engine had even been tried. Furthermore, tests at the Dunlop proving grounds in Birmingham produced the comment from development engineers that 'Speeds were the highest recorded so far for a Standard-Triumph model'. At that point, for sure, there were no qualms about the use of transverse leaf-spring swing axle rear suspension.

Construction of the first true Triumph-designed prototype began in the autumn of 1961, and a whole series of pictures in the archive show that this process spread over several months, from October to April 1962, while development was carried out on the first

car as the snags were discovered. It may seem amazing that the first proper prototype should not be ready until the spring of 1962, only six months before production began, but John Lloyd has pointed out that most of the actual structural work could be carried out on converted Heralds, and that only a successful pavé test of the completed body was essential.

Much work was done with a short-wheelbase Herald Convertible, which was painted battleship grey, and had one of the most disreputable hoods ever seen. It was in this car that the first 63 bhp 1147 cc engines were tried, and it was with this car that the author recalls carrying out endurance tests on the latest final drive assemblies. Almost all of the *Bomb* suspension and braking systems were pure Herald, in any case, except that there was no chassis outrigger to pick up the forward end of the rear

Not a vehicle to be proud of, the Standard Atlas was costly to develop. This is the 'Major'. Investment capital was wasted on this vehicle

radius arms (the body bulkhead behind the seats did that job on *Bomb*), and that spring and damper rates had to be retuned for the new, and considerably lighter, installation.

Keeping that phenomenal steering lock was never questioned. In spite of the fact that the maximum wheel 'back lock' was 50 degrees—a phenomenon which meant that ideal Ackermann-style geometry disappeared well before full lock was reached—any tyre scrub only occurred at very low road speeds. The turning circle of the Herald was remarkable enough, but that of the short-chassis Spitfire was even more so. *Autocar*'s 1962 test of the original production car showed that its turning circle between kerbs was a mere 24 ft 2 in., and that between walls (which allows for front overhang) it was 26 ft 0 in. No other car in the world, not even the familiar London taxi, could beat that.

Chassis number followers will want to know that the original Michelotti-built prototype carried the number X659—all Standard-Triumph cars carrying the prefix 'X' in a sequence initiated well before the Second World War. The first *Bomb* prototype built in Coventry, over the winter of 1961–2, was X691, later to be registered 4305VC; this car later had a very important part to play in the GT6 story, as we shall see. The prototype 'endurance' car, which followed a few weeks later, was X692, a red car registered in the spring of 1962 as 412VC. It was 412VC which later figured in many publicity pictures taken before the launch of the Spitfire, and eventually it was the very first Spitfire ever to be used by the competitions department, to be entered in British events to gain experience of modifications being finalized for the Le Mans and Alpine Rally team cars of 1964.

Very little significance should be attached to pictures of X691 being assembled with drum brake front suspension and a single carburettor engine, as these components were only fitted as 'slave' units while the alignment of the chassis frame was being checked out. What *was* of some importance, however, was that X692 (which became 412VC) was originally built with an instrument panel incorporating only a speedometer, a fuel gauge and a water temperature gauge, but without a rev counter; at this point, just before the specification was frozen, all efforts were being directed to getting unit costs down, and there was perhaps a sneaking feeling that the new car *might* be saleable at Midget prices after all. The car actually took to the road in this form in the early summer of 1962, but reverted to the familiar Mk 1 production specification in

time for publicity shots to be taken.

Other shots exist, too, of the red car posed against a variety of picturesque Warwickshire backgrounds without its full width bumper, and with only separate bumper over-riders covering the bonnet pivots. It was never seriously thought that the car should go on sale in this guise—the fact was that the proper chrome-plated bumper was not ready for fitment at this stage!

Time was now inexorably marching on, and if the necessary publicity material, advertisements, brochures, and service literature was to be ready in time for an eve-of-Show launch, *Bomb* would have to be christened. What should it be called?

Harry Webster has told me that he always wanted to keep the original code or project name, and market the car as the Triumph Bomb. More than once, in the 1960s, he would have liked this to happen—he finally got his way in 1970 when the *Stag* prototype went on the market with the same name. John Carpenter, Triumph's general sales manager at the time, cannot remember how *Spitfire* appeared, but suspects that it was all down to a brainwave from Donald Stokes, who began to make his presence felt at Coventry from mid-1961. Harry Webster, too, is certain that *Spitfire* was first suggested by the sales force but that, 'I wasn't sure how it would be received, because there might have been confusion with the Spitfire aircraft.' Even in those happy days, too, people occasionally worried about the use of such aggressive titles for cars, in case the do-gooders took exception to it.

No matter. Well before the middle of 1962, when plans were well ahead to start building Spitfire bodyshells at Forward Radiator, and when Sankeys were preparing to start building backbone chassis, *Bomb* was officially christened as *Spitfire*. More accurately, too, it was to be called *Spitfire 4*, and this is a title which has always attracted comment from uninformed observers who always stated firmly that it meant that there would soon be a *Spitfire 6* as well.

The truth of the matter was much more prosaic. By the time the Spitfire was ready for production, the six-cylinder Vitesse saloons and convertibles had gone on sale—these being yet further derivations of the basic Herald chassis. It was thought that the Americans would not be attracted to a car called the *Vitesse* when it went on sale in the United States, so for that market alone the car was re-named *Sports 6*. It wasn't actually a sports car, but it had a six-cylinder engine, and the name was thought to be good for possible sales. The new small sports car, which was about as different from the Vitesse as it could possibly be, needed a very different name. It was also thought essential to remind people that it had a four-cylinder engine. Logically, therefore, and without any more complicated reasoning than that, '4' was added to the generic name.

Experimental and development went ahead very smoothly. The author, by this time, was heavily involved in the build up of a re-opened competitions department and, apart from booking the use of the white car (X691—4305VC) as a 'chase' car for the RAC Rally, had very little to do with the *Bomb* project in its final stages. It rapidly became clear,

however, not only that it was a thoroughly enjoyable little car to drive (there was always a queue of skilled mechanics to take their turn at pushing the 'endurance' car round the long and testing route centred on Coventry which took in many Cotswolds roads, and took its name—the 'Birdlip route'—from the hill south of Cheltenham which figured strongly in it.), but that it was fast and strong as well. Pavé testing was relatively uneventful (all new Standard-Triumph cars were obliged to complete 1000 miles on the rough pavé roads at the MIRA proving ground, near Nuneaton, before being signed off for quantity production), and it also became clear that the welded-up bodyshell was much more leak-proof than the bolt-up shells used in Heralds and Vitesses.

Getting the handling right took rather longer. Fred Nicklin, who later had so much to do with the handling development of the competition cars,

---

Development was going apace on the 2 litre 6-cylinder engine soon to be used in the Triumph 2000 announced in October 1963

spent many hours testing the car with different springs and dampers—the whole object being to make the swing-axle rear suspension as versatile as possible. It was simpler in the case of the Spitfire than it had been with Herald and Vitesse, because the variation in load between the one-up, and two-up plus luggage conditions was not too severe; the maximum recommended payload for the Spitfire, indeed, was less than 400 lb. Nevertheless, it was a fact that the setting of the transverse leaf spring (and therefore the rear wheel) camber was critical. Tests showed that a 2.5 degree difference in rear wheel camber could be critical to roadholding and stability. According to the workshop manual issued for the original cars, the nominal rear wheel camber (unladen) should be five degrees positive, and then when laden it should be 3.5 degrees negative; furthermore, the production tolerance in the laden condition was only between three degrees and four degrees negative. To trim the handling as far as possible, it was decided to recommend tyre pressures of 18 psi (front) and 24 psi (rear), which was a considerable front-rear differential, intended to encourage a degree of understeer under all normal cornering conditions.

The car made ready for production was a fine product in most respects, but it also had some disappointing detail failings. For the sake of conformity with the Triumph Herald, the wheel rim width remained at a mere 3.5 in. the wide-ratio Herald gearbox was retained, and the 16 in. steering wheel used on the Herald 1200 was also used. It all took the edge off a fine basic design, and when I wrote my report after using 4305VC to follow the RAC Rally I made this clear. By this time, indeed, both Harry Webster and I realized that the Spitfire could be an excellent little competition car, and I wanted to be sure that the right features and accessories were eventually made available.

In the meantime, Leyland Motors—and Stanley Markland in particular—had set about transforming the Standard-Triumph business. Unsuccessful products like the Herald-engined Atlas van were scrapped, and the ambitious *Zero* tractor programme was abandoned. The slant-eyed Vitesse Six models went on sale in the summer of 1962, and the TR4 made a great start in North America. The ailing Vanguard Six was propped up by the simple but rugged 2.1-litre Standard Ensign, while the Herald saloons, estates, coupés, and convertibles were also joined by the Courier van.

It was an incredibly busy, and stimulating time, in the design and experimental departments, for while all this was going on, six-cylinder engines were being squeezed into TR4 structures, the Michelotti-proposed style for a new large saloon (*Barb*—eventually to become the Triumph 2000) was finalized, and much project work was done on Triumph's first front-wheel-drive saloon, known at the time as *Ajax*, but later to be officially named the Triumph 1300. There was even time for bizarre experiments to be carried out with the Herald-engined Amphicar (an amphibious car built in West Germany), and for an attempt to be made to put a Herald engine into a Vangard structure, to see if some sort of economy machine might be viable!

There was no time—literally, no time—for the Spitfire project to have lost its way, for any major development snag would have resulted in the October 1962 launch date having to be put back. In every way, however, the *Bomb*/Spitfire programme was a great success. Both Harry Webster (whose engineers designed it and John Lloyd (whose staff refined and developed it) remember how easy and straightforward it was to get the car ready for production. By the end of the summer, their job was done. The Spitfire *was* ready. But was it right for the market?

Chapter 3
Spitfires 1 and 2: 1962 to 1967

By any standards, the Spitfire was an important new car for Standard-Triumph to launch. A year earlier they had announced the TR4, a much more civilised car than the TR3A which it replaced, but now, only a year later, it had been matched by BMC with the release of the smoothly-styled monocoque MGB. At the same time, however, Triumph's new quality reputation was coming on apace, with the Herald 1200 seeming to better every week, and with the interesting six-cylinder Vitesse also making its mark.

Standard-Triumph did not rush in to reveal the Spitfire well in advance of the 1962 Earls Court Motor Show. Production cars, in any case, would not be ready for delivery to customers before the end of October, but much more important was the fact that several other very publicity-worthy new models (such as the Lotus Elan, the MGB, Jensen CV8, Morris 1100, and Ford Cortina) would also be making their bows in the weeks leading up to opening day. The actual launch of the Spitfire, therefore, was delayed until the very last minute, and only the privileged technical press got an earlier look at the little sports car.

BMC, incidentally, must have got wind of the impending arrival of the Spitfire, for they made frenzied last-minute efforts to improve the Sprite and Midget models to cope with the direct new threat. When the Spitfire was being developed, Spridgets still had 948 cc, drum brakes all round, and 46 bhp (net)/50 bhp (gross). The 1963 models, rushed out on the very eve of the show, and quite overshadowed by the interest being shown in the Spitfire, had longer-stroke 1098 cc engines, front-wheel disc brakes, and 55 bhp (net) engines. They were still lumbered with sliding sidescreens and a narrow cockpit, however, the result being that the Spitfire still appeared to be a better car in almost every respect.

There was no doubt about the Spitfire's reception. Almost everyone, except BMC and their dealers, seemed to be impressed. Standard-Triumph's advertising, written weeks earlier, had already decided that this would be so for their copy trumpeted, 'Where's the biggest crowd at the Motor Show? Round the new Triumph Spitfire 4, brushing up their ideas on how lively and how luxurious a low-price sports car can be. . .' As for the press, Ronald 'Steady' Barker, writing his annual *Autocar* show-time 'gossip-column' about the exhibits, had this to say, which was a typical reaction.

'Another fresh sports car is the Triumph Spitfire. . . . This has a form of backbone chassis, which can be examined in detail on the stand. It has a much shorter wheelbase than the Herald, and a welded-together body. Horner (the artist illustrating the feature: AAGR) thought it looked rather feminine, a difficult adjective to define in this context; perhaps we would have preferred less sweep and more angle. Barker, who has driven a Spitfire, likes its almost dainty, responsive handling and very smooth engine—you could almost mistake it for a six—and the real punch at low engine speeds, which is scarcely a feature of the Herald saloons. It is very civilised, with winding windows and plenty of luggage space, and £730 for a 90-plus mph car

ABOVE RIGHT: Autocar's cutaway drawing of the Spitfire shows the compact layout of the new small Standard-Triumph sports car, particularly the detail of the backbone frame and suspensions. Note the large space ahead of the cooling radiator

RIGHT: After 412VC had completed its work as a prototype in the summer of 1962, it became a publicity vehicle. This was a high-speed shot used in several advertisements

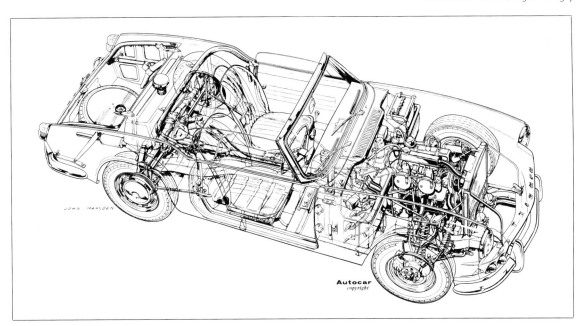

seems reasonable enough. It should, as they say, go far as well as fast.'

A beautifully presented display chassis—mechanically complete, but without bodywork—was on the Triumph stand, while nearby a white car rotated serenely on a turntable. Unhappily for BMC, one feels, the MG stand was right alongside the Triumph exhibits, where the little-changed Midget had to fight with the Spitfire, and with its own stable-mate the MGB, for what little attention it could get.

The display chassis showed that much of the suspension layout was familiar, drew attention to the front-wheel disc brakes, and showed the remarkably-detailed front suspension layout which allowed such a phenomenal steering lock to be developed. It also showed that although the 1147 cc engine was basically that of the Herald 1200, and although a single-outlet cast-iron exhaust manifold had been retained, twin 1.25 in. SU HS2 carburettors, new manifolding, a 9.0:1 compression ratio, and a more sporting high-lift camshaft, had combined to raise peak power from the 39 bhp of the Herald to no less than 63 bhp (net) at 5750 rpm.

Neither could there be any criticism of access to the engine bay. Getting at the engine of the Sprite/ Midget cars was much worse than it had been with the original Sprite, where the entire nose hinged up from the scuttle. With the Spitfire, it was difficult to see how access could be improved at all. On the very first cars there were no engine bay side curtains (these were to be added later), and on all cars the bonnet could not only be swung up from its nose pivots, but with no more than a little disconnecting on electrical leads to the lamps, it could be removed altogether.

The seating, the instrumentation, and the general cockpit layout were quite superb, and much better than the appointments offered on the Spridget. Dimensionally, the Spitfire was a couple of inches wider between the doors, provided 2.5 in. more arm room between the steering wheel and the seat back rest, provided 2.5 in. more leg room between pedals

RIGHT: *There was not a jarring line anywhere on the Spitfire—a real tribute to Michelotti's genius*

BELOW: *412VC was a hard-working little car, and even though it was hand-built it shows off the finalised lines of the Spitfire to good effect*

and seats, and no less than five inches longer front leg tunnels to allow the passenger to stretch out. With more stowage space behind the seats, and a considerably larger boot, not forgetting the provision of an 8.25 (Imp.) gallon fuel tank with a massive central filler (the Spridget had a mere six gallons, and a smaller filler tucked down by the tail), emerged as a much better all-round proposition.

Overall, the Spitfire's performance matched that of the up-engined Midget in all respects. Their sprint times to the $\frac{1}{4}$-mile were virtually identical, as were their 0–60 and 0–80 mph times. Fuel consumption figures (always difficult to quantify when different drivers use different cars at different times) were marginally to the Spitfire's advantage, and its top speed of around 93 mph was at least three more than the Midget could achieve. There remained, of course, the matter of price—the only area where the BMC product could claim an advantage. The Spitfire was so well-equipped, in fact, that it simply had to sell at a slightly higher price than the Spridgets, though this never did it any harm. On announcement, the basic British price of the Spitfire

was £530 (Total, with tax, £730), which compared with £485 for the Sprite and £495 for the mechanically identical Midget. However, even while talk of the motor show was still dying down, an autumn budget resulted in a reduction of purchase tax from 55 per cent to 25 per cent of wholesale prices, which meant that the Spitfire found itself selling for £641, which was a mere £42 (or seven per cent) more than that asked for the Midget. It was no

RIGHT: *One of the first 1962 Spitfires. Don't be misled by the number plate, which was false. 5VC actually belonged to one of the works TR4 rally cars*

BELOW RIGHT: *If you own an early-model Spitfire of 1962 or 1963, its fascia and foot wells should look like this; only the gear lever gaiter is non-standard (it should be black). The floor covering was moulded rubber*

BELOW: *With the hood erected, a Mk I Spitfire's lines were not quite as elegant*

wonder, therefore, that demand for the Spitfire boomed from the day it was revealed. The dealers loved it, the customers were already rushing to order their Spitfires, and every Standard-Triumph estimate of its potential sales hastily had to be revised—upwards.

It is appropriate, at this moment, to make it quite clear that the Spitfire consistently outsold the Sprite/Midget models throughout the next two decades. Spitfire lovers must always have suspected as much, but as there always seems to have been a well-orchestrated attempt by some historians to prove that the Abingdon-built cars were the most popular ever to have been seen in the world of motoring, it has never been made clear.

The facts, however, are crystal clear. The Spitfire and the Sprite/Midget models were in close, and direct, competition, from 1963 to 1979, at which

point the Midget was finally dropped. In every calendar year except one—1969—more Spitfires were built and sold than the total of Sprites and Midgets added together. Even in 1969, when Standard-Triumph was afflicted by a strike for some time, the shortfall of Spitfire sales were a mere 640 cars in 19,000. This is proof positive, surely, that the Spitfire, and its marketing approach, was always well in tune with the buying public's needs, even though only a single 'badge' was available?

Certainly there was never any lack of interest in the Spitfire at first, even in North America, where most of the early production cars went into filling up the supplies 'pipe-line' before the car could formally be launched early in 1963. Even today, nearly 20 years after it happened, I can recall the way in which my Spitfire 'chase car' was instantly surrounded by spectators whenever it stopped at, or near, a control on the International RAC Rally of that year. Hindsight suggests that a superior approach to the business had been developing at BMC for some years, and lovers of small sports cars were delighted to be given a real choice at last.

Earls Court Motor Show display chassis of the original Mk I Spitfire. No other Spitfire was ever as smart as this!

I have to say that, accompanied by tester Fred Nicklin on my 2000-mile dash around the country, I found quite a lot that I would have liked to see improved, and my report to management suggested that the biggest single improvement would be to specify the close-ratio Vitesse gearbox instead of the rather wide-ratio Herald variety. Neither box, of course, had a synchronized first gear, but at the time that wasn't considered too important.

It wasn't only the formal magazine tests which showed how much the technical press of Britain and North America liked the Spitfire, the more relaxed features written around the same period did to. In a very revealing study, *The Motor*'s Joe Lowrey, a very distinguished and perceptive technical editor, talked about a quick trip he had just made to Turin for the motor show in that city. It was not that he made the journey in a Spitfire, which was interesting enough, but that two Spitfires were involved, and that Lowrey's companions included Harry Webster, John Lloyd, and George Turner (managing director of Alford and Alder). The two cars were 3607VC and 3609VC—both very early pilot-build

production cars—and it was the sort of trip which is always invaluable to top engineers, when they have time to re-examine the car they have designed under long-distance driving conditions.

There was no doubting Lowrey's feelings about the car, particularly its comfort when faced with wintry conditions in the Alps between France and Italy. At the end of a difficult day, in Turin, after having to retreat from a snow-blocked Col du Mont Cenis, he commented that, 'In sharp contrast with the way one used to get out of a sports car, we emerged from the winding-window, centrally heated Spitfires clean and dry after a lot of miles in cool showery weather.' Clearly there had been a lot of time for opinions about the car, its plus points, and its failings, to be discussed, for Lowrey sounded off enthusiastically about the handling ('Both of them felt true sports cars, cornering fast without

Room and to spare in the Spitfire Mk I's engine bay, but no splash guards at each side just yet

body roll or excitement and responding to a finger-light touch on the steering wheel') even if he was clearly not quite as convinced about the use of swing-axle independent rear suspension as he might have been. It was the sort of trip, too, in which engineers begin to realize where they have gone wrong, even in a minor way, for Lowrey's opening remarks were that, 'Very soon now, the Triumph Spitfire will probably have a modified parcel shelf on its fascia, guaranteed not to release an avalanche of maps upon the passenger's lap when the driver accelerates hard. This is the sort of small but by no means unimportant improvement to a new model which happens much more quickly when designers really use their own products than when a car factory's head men go everywhere by air.' This got to the nub of the matter very directly, for Harry Webster was a car driving enthusiast in every way, and not just a designer of distinction. At first, the Spitfire was his baby, and he made sure it stayed that way.

The Motor, in its formal road test, had been enthusiastic about the Spitfire (3609VC—one of the two 'Turin-trip' cars), calling it an 'outstanding new small sports car', and describing its road-holding as 'outstanding'. The last must have been something of a generalization as their analysis in the text mentioned that, 'as the cornering limit is approached, the tail "hangs out" and a little steering has to be paid off, after which the chosen line will be followed closely.' Another cautionary note in their report was that they thought the interior trim too spartan.

The standard of furnishing, indeed, was something of a talking point inside Standard-Triumph, for there was no doubt that the rubber mats, the areas of exposed sheet metal in body colour, and the rather slim and basic seats, could all have been improved if the sales force had agreed to cost increases as well. The problem was that the rest of the car set such high standards—in performance, in styling, and in behaviour. Somehow one was likely to accept such finish in a BMC car which jumped from crag to crag on hard damper settings, and offered no luxury in terms of ventilation, heating, and stowage space, but on a Spitfire it didn't seem right. For the future, therefore, something would have to be done.

Evocative publicity shot with the legendary Supermarine Spitfire fighter (a Mk Vb, AB910, built in 1941 and still flying in 1982) in the background and—if I may say so—dominating the shot

On the other hand, there was so much to be happy about—that phenomenally tight turning circle, the economy (35 to 40 mpg Imp., if you worked at it—but few owners did!), the styling, and the public demand for the car—that the engineers did not need to contemplate major changes for some time to come.

The immediate problem as far as magazine testers were concerned (but not, apparently, as far as buyers were concerned) was that the rear suspension was simply not up to its job. Every Triumph executive I have spoken to says that the behaviour of the rear suspension was never a resistance to sales, and that in the end it was necessary for a very low-cost change to be developed before any modification was approved; this, however, did not impress the testers. Perhaps *Road & Track*, in their April 1963 road test, put it best of all, 'When pressed along at racing speeds . . . the high roll centre caused the back of the car to lift, and the wheels begin to pull under, which sends the rear of the car skating sharply outward. The Spitfire's quick, precise, steering makes it easy to catch the car before the situation gets out of hand, but it is impossible to get round a race course very rapidly. . . . Also, on tight corners, the inside rear wheel lifts completely clear of the road and spins free. . . .

Motoring Life, of Dublin, asked, 'How can these bus builders do it at the price?' and the tester also commented that, 'All I am prepared to state is that the man who, after covering a reasonable mileage in the Spitfire, still sees fit to complain, must be a first-class misery.'

As far as the production engineers at Canley were concerned, the first two years of Spitfire assembly were all about building as many cars as possible. At a time when corporate production was reaching for 3000 cars a week, 400 of them were Spitfires. More, no doubt, could have been sold at this early stage, but the body tooling at Forward Radiator was quite incapable of producing any more shells.

The engineers, in the meantime, were encouraged not to think about changing the Spitfire completely, but to look for ways to improve it in detail. They were, however, persuaded by the Jack Brabham organization (who were already offering

412VC again—this time with Harry Webster (left) and George Turnbull also taking a bow. At this stage in its life, the car had left-hand drive, but it started as a right-hand-drive machine, and reverted to right-hand-drive for rallying use in 1964!

Herald-Climax conversions) to instal a 1216 cc Coventry-Climax FWE engine in a development car to see if such a 'marriage' would work properly. The car chosen for the transplant was 3607VC—the yellow pilot production car carrying Chassis No. 2, which had accompanied *The Motor*'s road test car to Turin the previous November.

To no-one's surprise, the installation was straightforward enough (one of the benefits of the separate chassis design was how versatile it was), and the performance benefits were considerable. Top speed rose to 105 mph, and the standing quarter mile sprint time was reduced to 18.2 seconds. It was a short-lived experiment, however, not only because such a car would have had to carry a high price in the showrooms, but because the life of the FWE engine was also likely to be limited by the demise of its major user, the Lotus Elite. In addition, the department had also been testing the original versions of what eventually became the 'Stage II' tuning kit on the basis of the 1147 cc Spitfire, and

had proved to be even quicker than the Climax-engined car. The whole story of Spitfire tuning kits, however, is closely tied up with the racing and rallying development story, and is covered in more detail as a special section in this Chapter.

RIGHT: *In the autumn of 1963, a detachable hardtop was made available for the Spitfire, as an option. This was then unchanged until the launch of the Mk IV in 1970/71*

BELOW RIGHT: *The Spitfire's boot space, with scissor jack stowed to one side, the fuel tank over the rear wheels (behind the trim panel), and with hood sticks stowed around the tank, and held in place by the leather strap*

BELOW: *Smile and breathe in, please! Which rather diverts attention from the Spitfire (Price £729 15s 3d) at the 1962 Earls Court Motor Show*

The development changes announced in time for the 1964 model year were all very welcome, and functional. The centre-lock wire spoke wheels being tested on 3607VC at the time it made the Turin trip in November 1962 became optional, as did a smart detachable steel hardtop. Of even more importance, however, was the offering of overdrive (to operate on top and third gears) as an option, not merely because it made the prospect of an economical little car even more economical, but because it was a feature not offered (and never to be offered, in fact) on the Sprite/Midget models.

The public's response was immediate. Sales in 1963 exceeded 20,000 for the first time, but in 1964 they raced ahead to 23,387 units. In the face of this popularity, not even the revamped Sprites and Midgets (which, in 1964 were fitted with winding windows, revised fascias, and boosted 59 bhp engines) could compete, and the Spitfire won the sales battle again.

In that same year, too, Triumph took their much-modified Spitfires to Le Mans, where they finished with honour, and to the Tour de France, where one of the team rally cars defeated every Alpine-Renault and Bonnet (Renault), works or privately-owned, which had been entered. The car was on the crest of a wave, and Standard-Triumph were not going to allow the impetus, and the growing reputation, to slip away.

The result, in March 1965, was that the Spitfire Mk 2 was revealed. On this occasion, as on others in the years to come, the Spitfire was updated at the same time as new features were added to the Triumph TR series, but on this occasion it was quite overshadowed by the new all-independent suspension chassis which denoted the change from TR4 to TR4A.

Compared with the original Spitfire, now retrospectively to be known as the Mk 1, the Spitfire Mk 2 had a little more power, and rather more refinement in cockpit fittings and details. No more was needed to sustain the popularity of the car. A sale, after all, of 45,753 Mk 1 Spitfires in little more than two full years was highly satisfying. The changes to the 1147 cc engine comprised the use of a revised camshaft profile, a water-cooled inlet manifold, and a fabricated tubular exhaust manifold, all of which combined to improve the breathing, and to increase peak power from 63 bhp to 67 bhp (net) at 6000 rpm. A Borg and Beck diaphragm spring clutch was standardized (this change was progressively being made—to oust the coil spring variety—throughout the British motor industry), and all the established options were continued.

More comfortably looking seat trims (on the same frames) were fitted, and there had been a general attempt to get rid of most of the exposed surfaces in the cockpit by covering them with leather cloth. Most important of all was that the moulded rubber floor coverings of the original car had given way to moulded carpets, and this—at a stroke—not only made the car look richer and more welcoming, but it also worked wonders for the general refinement of travel.

The writer, who had been directing the fortunes of the competitions department while the first series of Spitfires were in production, took delivery of a 1964 model, and thoroughly enjoyed its behaviour, nimble behaviour in traffic, and its economy. I always regret ordering it without overdrive, but the reason for this was quite simple—that I could not afford the extra money.

The Spitfire, like its rivals, was not really a single model, but one on which the options could be piled up if the customer wanted it that way. The Mk 2, incidentally, was priced at £550 (basic) when introduced in 1965 (Austin-Healey Sprite £505, MG Midget £515), and in the summer of 1966, when *Autocar* came to test the latest car that price had not changed. To the total price of £677.76, however, had to be added £58.38 for the overdrive, £36.88 for the centre-lock wire wheels, £9.83 for radial ply tyres, £13.52 for the fresh-air heater, £29.58 for the pushbutton radio, and £9.45 for the static seat belts. There was no hardtop on the test car, which would have added £33.83 to the growing total. It was not that there was anything dishonest about the original pricing, but that there were so many different extras available, and so many different owners' requirements to be satisfied.

The Mk 2 did not achieve the claimed 96 mph in *Autocar*'s hands (it actually achieved 92 in direct top, with overdrive top a little slower), but it had cut the

---

ABOVE RIGHT: *Triumph's new Canley assembly hall, finished in 1960/61 for the expansion in Herald production, the home of every Spitfire built between 1962 and 1980, now gutted for other purposes*

RIGHT: *The cockpit of the Spitfire Mk 2, like that of the Mk 1 except for the use of carpeted floors, the covering up of all previously-exposed painted metal surfaces, and for more luxuriously styled seats*

ABOVE: *The Spitfire's swing-axle suspension was always supported by a very robust 'bridge' at the rear of the chassis frame*

ABOVE RIGHT: *Knock-on, centre-lock wire-spoke wheels were introduced as an option in 1963, and were a popular fitting. The option was finally withdrawn in 1973*

TOP: *The show chassis in Mk 2 form, showing the backbone shape of the frame and general layout*

BELOW RIGHT: *The discreet chrome script on the boot lid tells us that this was one of the many Mk 2 Spitfires fitted with overdrive—something never ever offered by Abingdon*

0–60 mph time to 15.5 sec., and was clearly a more lively car in all respects. The most remarkable figures, however, were those achieved at constant speeds in overdrive top. At 30 mph fuel was eked out at the rate of 58.9 mpg, at 50 mph 50.0 mpg, and at 70 mph (the motorway speed limit just about to be introduced) consumption was still a mere 38.1 mpg. The fact that *Autocar*'s overall test figure was 29.8 mpg shows just how hard all the testers were driving the lastest Spitfire. I recall that I was on the

magazine's staff by this time, and I can still remember the enthusiasm generated among other drivers. The text confirms this, for the rear suspension (which was well down on this test car) was praised heartily, as were most of the new features. Only the hard ride, and the build-it-yourself hood and sticks called for reproach.

No matter. By this time there was a lot going for the Spitfire, especially as it was about to be joined by 'Big Brother', the six-cylinder-engined GT6 coupé, and because it had made such a fine reputation for itself in two short seasons of 'works' competition. Production and sales were still limited by Forward Radiator's (and Canley's) inability to build any more cars—which was a far cry from the desperate days of 1960–61 when Standard-Triumph was dying rapidly for lack of sales. As it was, final assembly of Spitfires—after the backbone chassis had been mated to the bodyshell—began with the structure sideways across the tracks, and with work being carried out under the front and rear of the chassis at the same time. It was only towards the end of the process, near the northern end of the new Canley assembly hall, that the mixed line of Spitfires, Heralds, Vitesses and (later) GT6s began to crawl towards completion in a conventional attitude.

In the meantime, sales of Sprites and Midgets were slipping badly—in 1966 17,077 Spitfires were sold, compared with a mere 13,866 Sprites and Midgets combined—and BMC made another move to restore the balance. From the autumn of 1966, in a move long discounted by the pundits, BMC installed a productionized 1275 Cooper S engine in place of the long-stroke 1098 cc unit, which had the effect of pushing up the Spridget's power from 59 bhp to 64 bhp, and of making a much more tuneable proposition out of the car. Functionally, the most important BMC change was the fitting of a fold-away hood and sticks for the first time, but then it brought their prices up to those of the Spitfire (£545 for the Sprite, and £555 for the Midget, against £550 for the Spitfire).

Not that this seemed to perturb Standard-Triumph's management, for the new GT6 was making plenty of headlines, and demand for the Spitfire did not slacken. In any case, if BMC had only known it, they were already pitching against an obsolete model, for important changes were planned for the Spitfire in 1967.

All these Spitfire and GT6 changes were completed to a tight time schedule in spite of a heavy involvement in competition motoring which began (for the Spitfire) in 1963 and ended in 1966. It was a short but technically fascinating period, which taught the engineers a lot about their cars, and produced much favourable publicity. So much happened, and so much was learned, that the Spitfire competitions programme deserves a chapter of its own.

Final assembly of Spitfires, at one point, was mixed with that of Heralds, Vitesses and GT6s, and the cars travelled sideways, to allow easy access to front and rear suspension

Factory 'Tune-Up' kits

Even before the factory-backed Spitfire competitions programme went ahead, Standard-Triumph were already thinking of offering tune-up kits for the new Spitfire. The fact that the Spitfire could not be made competitive without a great deal of new equipment, which had to be on offer to the public, made the development of kits imperative. By the beginning of 1964, therefore, and in spite of the fact that parts were in extremely short supply for some time afterwards, a range of three engine conversions were made available.

These were dubbed Interim, Stage I and Stage II, with the Stage II kit approximating to, but being by no means the same as, that used on the factory-built race and rally team cars of 1964 and 1965. No factory literature about these kits survives

today, but I have been able to draw on a feature I prepared for the *Standard-Triumph Review* of February 1964 to recall the details.

The **Interim** conversion comprised an exchange high-compression (9.75 : 1) cylinder head, a downdraught Solex compound dual choke Type 32PAIA carburettor, new inlet and four-branch exhaust manifolds, and was slated as producing 70 bhp. The cost was £47 16s. 1d.

You might think that this is a craftsman shaping an original Spitfire model, but look at the artist's sketches in the background, which are of the 1970/71 model Spitfire Mk IV!

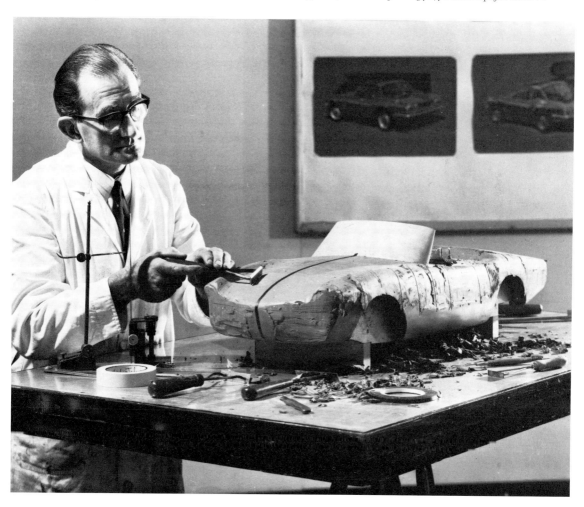

Stage I My feature described this as having, 'A completely new cylinder head, having individual inlet and exhaust ports and a compression ratio of 10.5:1, together with different carburation and a fabricated exhaust manifold. The specifications also include a new high-lift camshaft together with valves and valve gear to suit. The power output of this conversion is approximately 80 bhp, and it is recommended that in addition to the above, stronger pistons and connecting rods are fitted (these are available as separate items).

The snag is that the type of carburettor *was never mentioned*, and memory suggests that work had not even started on the conversion when those words were written, and I doubt if any were ever sold. However, I also remember that Roy Fidler's 'development' competition Spitfire (412VC—see Chapter 4), started at least one British event with a single dual-choke Weber carburettor installation which approximated to what Stage I was all about. Nevertheless, it was priced at £92 5s. 0d.

Stage II This was the important tune-up kit, of which 100 sets had to be made to convince the motor sporting authorities that the 'team' Spitfires were fit to be homologated. Without that proof, or the readiness to give proof, there would have been no racing or rallying programme in 1964 and 1965. The fact that the cast-iron head used on the team cars was not the same casting as that offered in the Stage II kit was never mentioned, nor that the cast-alloy head used by the rallying Spitfires in 1964 and by some race cars in 1965 was never offered for sale is no longer important. At the time, we all shrugged this off on the grounds that every other competing factory (and, most especially, Ford and BMC) were up to the same sort of tricks.

A limited number of 'Stage II' Spitfires were sold in 1964 and 1965, with twin-choke Weber carburettors and tubular exhaust manifolds

The 'customer' Stage II conversion, in fact, was well on the way before the factory's racing programme was even mooted, for speed tests of a prototype installation were carried out by Fred Nicklin in May 1963 when a top speed of 107 mph was achieved at MIRA.

The major components of the Stage II kit were a new 'eight-port' cylinder head (and 10.5:1 compression ratio), two dual-choke Weber Type 40DCOE carburettors, new inlet manifolds, four-branch exhaust manifolds, a high-lift camshaft (different from Stage I, I wrote about in 1964), and other details. This was priced at £179 0s. 0d. (and don't forget that a Spitfire, in 1964, cost a mere £641!), and you had to pay extra for the stronger pistons, connecting rods, crankshaft, diaphragm spring clutch and Vitesse close-ratio gears which were almost essential to make a meaningful kit out of it all. The claimed power output, however, was 90 bhp at 6500 rpm, which for some people made it all worth while.

I should make it clear that the factory only ever made such kits available because they thought it was expected of them (and, in the case of the Stage II kit, it was necessary for homologation purposes), and that their hearts were never truly in it. Distribution rights were placed with SAH Accessories of Leighton Buzzard, and I doubt if more than a score of each type of conversion (Interim or Stage II) were ever delivered. But who knows today? The factory certainly do not, neither do the luminaries from SAH, which changed hands some years ago.

For the record, these are the performance summaries claimed by the factory for Spitfires with these kits fitted;

The 'Interim' tuning kit listed for Spitfires in 1964 and 1965, with a tubular exhaust manifold like Stage II cars, but with special inlet manifold and a downdraught Solex twin-choke compound carburettor

Standard	Max. 92 mph, 0–60 mph 15.5 sec., standing start $\frac{1}{4}$-mile 19.5 sec.
Interim	Max. 96 mph, 0–60 mph 13 sec., standing start $\frac{1}{4}$-mile 19.2 sec.
Stage I	Max. 102 mph, 0–60 mph 12 sec., standing start $\frac{1}{4}$-mile 18.7 sec.
Stage II	Max. 107 mph, 0–60 mph 10.6 sec., standing start $\frac{1}{4}$-mile 18.3 sec.

In addition, and to prove their point, Standard-Triumph built up a demonstration car (registered 3139KV), with a full-house Stage II conversion installed, and loaned it to *Autocar* for test. The report, published in the issue of 12 February 1965 (one week after the engine development story written by the author and Ray Bates of the factory design staff had been published), was a real eye-opener for those who did not think Spitfires should go so fast!

Acceleration figures were very slightly down on those claimed by the factory (0–60 mph took 11.2 sec., while the maximum speed was 104 mph), but the remarkable improvements were obvious. To 80 mph, for instance, the Stage II car took 20.9 sec., while the standard 1962 Spitfire I had taken no less than 36.9 sec., and even this was considered fully competitive at the time. The test car not only had the engine and transmission parts installed, but came complete with modified springs, dampers, and wide-rim wheels (the homologated 4.5 in. Courier van variety), and was stated as costing £972.

Autocar's testers thought that, 'From a sweet little two-seater tourer it becomes a rorty little ball of fire', and a further extract from their writings is fascinating.

'Below about 2700 rpm there is very little torque—not surprising with the peak of this curve at 4900 rpm, and maximum revs over 7000 rpm... The engine revs smoothly and so freely that one needs to keep a wary eye on the rev counter... Although there is a lot of noise in the cockpit... outside observers told us that it did not cause a nuisance. A lot of deep induction roar makes the car sound potent, and there is a snarl from the exhaust that is crisp and angry in tone....

'Handling of the car is much improved by the modified suspension and radial ply tyres... This is where the Stage II Spitfire becomes a real "fun" car if one feels in the mood for some sporting driving... Everyone on our staff who drove the test car came back looking years younger and full of enthusiasm for it. We would readily add it to our stable if funds permitted, as a means of relieving depression; someone even suggested it should be available on the National Health...'

The Stage II Spitfire, indeed, could be a really exhilarating car, and in out-and-out 'works' team guise the developed car could be truly inspiring, as any of the team's drivers would confirm.

Facts and figures: Spitfire 4 (now universally called 'Mk 1')
General specification

All Spitfires and GT6 models built between 1962 and 1980 were based on the same basic design, engine/chassis/body layout. The following features were common throughout the range of models: Separate box-section steel backbone-style chassis frame, with front-mounted engine/transmission, and rear chassis-mounted final drive unit. Pressed steel two-seater bodyshell—open sports car with optional detachable hardtop for all Spitfires, fastback coupé hatchback style for all GT6s.

Independent front suspension, by coil springs, wishbones, telescopic dampers, and anti-roll bar. Rack and pinion steering.
Independent rear suspension by transverse leaf spring, radius arms and telescopic dampers; swing axles and minor differences between models; lower wishbone location on some GT6 models.
Girling front wheel disc brakes, rear wheel drums; minor differences between models.
Wheelbase, all models, 83 in. (211 cm.)

Spitfire 4

Built October 1962 to December 1964
Number built 45,573
Chassis numbers FC 1 to FC 44656 inclusive, with left-hand-drive cars recognised by an 'L' suffix

Engine 4-cyl., in-line, cast-iron cylinder block and cylinderhead, with three crankshaft main bearings. Bore, stroke and capacity 69.3 × 76 mm., 1147 cc (2.73 × 2.99 in., 70 cu. in.). CR 9.0:1, 2 SU carburettors. 63 bhp at 5750 rpm. Maximum torque 67 lb. ft at 3500 rpm.

Transmission Final drive ratio 4.11:1. Overall gear ratios 4.11 (3.37 in optional overdrive top), 5.74, 8.88, 15.42, reverse 15.42:1. Synchromesh on top, third and second gears. Overdrive (on top and third gears) optional from September 1963. 15.7 mph/1000 rpm in direct top gear; 19.1 mph/1000 rpm in overdrive top gear.

Basic prices UK £530
USA $2199

Suspension and brakes 9.0 in. front disc brakes, 7 × 1.25 in. rear drums. 520-13 in. tyres on 3.5 in. rim bolt-on steel disc wheels or 4.5 in. rim centre-lock wire-spoke wheels.

Dimensions Length 12 ft 1 in.; width 4 ft 9 in.; height 3 ft 11.5 in. Front track 4 ft 1 in.; rear track 4 ft 0 in. Unladen weight (basic specification) 1568 lb.

Spitfire Mk 2

Built December 1964 to January 1967
Number built 37,409
Chassis numbers FC 50001 to FC 88904 inclusive, with left-hand-drive cars recognised by an 'L' suffix

Basic prices UK £550
USA $2199

Technical specification as for Spitfire 4 (Mk 1) except for: Engine: 67 bhp at 6000 rpm. Maximum torque 67 lb. ft at 3750 rpm.

Chapter 4
Big budget: the works competition cars

Just before Christmas 1961, Harry Webster called me into his office at Coventry, and told me that he thought Standard-Triumph's competition programme should be started again, and that he wanted me to run it. It was all going to be different from the last time, he said—there would be a lot less money to spend, and he would be in direct control. It was one in which the Spitfire came to be honed into a formidable little machine.

Standard-Triumph's first serious involvement in competitions began with Ken Richardson in 1953. Richardson eventually ran what was virtually a self-contained operation from a variety of homes, concentrating mainly on the use of Triumph TRs, and eventually running the twin-cam engined TR3S and TRS Le Mans prototypes. In 1961, however (even though the TRSs had just won the Team Prize at Le Mans), S-T's new owners, Leyland Motors, decreed that all competition activity had to stop, to save money. The team was dispersed, and Richardson left the company virtually overnight.

That policy, however, was soon reversed, for the sales force wanted to see Triumph cars back in competitions, and Harry Webster himself was an avowed motor racing enthusiast. For the first two years, however, the budget was so restricted that it was only feasible to use the tried and tested TRs (by now TR4s and for the first time in substantially tuned and lightened form), but by the autumn of 1963 it was clear that big decisions were needed.

Further discussion with Harry Webster helped to identify three possible courses of action for 1964, a season in which it was known that the first two British 'homologation specials'—the Mini-Cooper S and the Ford Lotus-Cortina would reach maturity. The alternatives were:

1 To carry on rallying TR4s, which were becoming uncompetitive.

2 To close the department down.

3 To expand considerably and develop competition versions of the new Spitfire and 2000 models.

To Webster's eternal credit, he rejected the first two alternatives, and recommended expansion to his fellow directors. He admitted privately to me, he dearly wanted to take Triumph back to Le Mans again, and thought that a super-tuned Spitfire might surprise a lot of people.

Board approval was gained in December 1963 (*after* work had already begun!), and every design department was involved. The Spitfires would race at Le Mans, and would rally in tarmac events like the Alpine and the Tour de France; the strong Triumph 2000s were to specialize as 'rough-road' cars, on events like Liège-Sofia-Liège and the RAC Rallies. The first event for the 2000 to tackle was not to take place until August 1964, so all preliminary work could be concentrated on the Spitfire.

The Spitfire's competition class, when homologated for racing and rallying, was the 1.3-litre category of Group 3 (Grand Touring), which meant that its obvious competition would come from the deadly British rival, the MG Midget/Austin-Healey Sprite as well as the more specialized little machines like the rear-engined Alpine-Renaults and Fiat

---

Abarths, and mid-engined Bonnet (Renault). In addition, and where the regulations allowed it, this group could also be expanded to include 1.3-litre saloons modified beyond the limits of their own

Group 2—and that meant that cars like the Mini-Cooper S and (soon) the Renault 8 Gordini could also become Spitfire opposition.

At Le Mans, however, the Spitfires would have to be entered as prototypes, which allowed more or less any or every modification to be made to their basic design. It was within these two sets of parameters, and with a very encouraging budget (of the order of *eight times*, nominally, that available to go rallying with TR4s), not to mention the enthusiastic support of almost every department of the Standard-Triumph business, that planning for 1964 began.

Quite clearly, the standard Spitfire was not fast enough to be competitive. To transform it into a 'real racer', therefore, it was necessary—(a) to make it much faster; more power, better aerodynamics, less weight and; (b) to improve its roadholding and braking—all, mark you, without ruining its reliability prospects. In addition, because the rally cars would have to be 'homologated' (they had to comply with a fairly strict set of rules, and that some special equipment had to be made available to the

LEFT: *The Le Mans Spitfire's first appearance in public was at Oulton Park, for testing, in April 1964. Fred Nicklin is here seen flogging the car around the Cheshire circuit. The Le Mans style of bonnet has not yet been fitted*

BELOW LEFT: *At the initial Oulton Park test session, Peter Bolton (with coffee cup), David Hobbs (centre) and the author (then competitions secretary of Standard-Triumph) discuss the car's behaviour*

BELOW: *One of the two normal-bonneted Spitfire Le Mans cars at the practice weekend in France, in April 1964. The competition number, painted on, had not stood up to the wet weather! The restricted radiator air intake had already been developed*

general public), many unwelcome compromises would have to be made.

Making the Spitfire faster was a pure engineering problem, solved perfectly competently, if not quickly or easily, by developing an entirely new eight-port cylinder head, new camshaft profiles, carburation by twin-choke Weber carburettors, and efficiently gas-flowed inlet and exhaust manifolds. A look at the performance of other 1.3-litre cars at Le Mans in 1963 suggested that the new Spitfires would need to be able to lap at up to 100 mph (in other words, they would have to be as fast as the 2-litre TRS prototypes had been in 1961!), and that would dictate a top speed of at least 130 mph. On the

assumption that the shape of the car could be improved, it was thought that a 100 bhp output would do the job.

Getting that sort of power was easier said than done. It required a specific output of 87 bhp/litre *to be maintained over a 24 hour period*, and produced from the bare bones of a production-based cylinder block, three-bearing crankshaft, and narrow main bearings. In short, producing the power by means of an efficient new cylinder head (the standard Spitfire was lumbered with siamezed inlet ports) and valve gear was relatively straight-forward, but making such an engine reliable was not. It was to the great credit of Standard-Triumph engineers that the task was successfully completed in less than six months, without the need to call in outside specialists, and without the need of a sophisticated dry sump lubrication system, or exotic crankshaft and connecting rod materials. The 70X engine (as it was known internally—70 being the engine capacity in cubic inches, X merely meaning eXperimental) eventually beat its 100 bhp target by a comfortable margin, became available in cast-iron or light-alloy cylinder head form, and was docile enough for a Spitfire rally car to be driven slowly through city traffic.

Developing the right aerodynamic shape proved to be easier still. Webster wanted to be sure that his race cars would be instantly recognizable as

LEFT: *One of the original Spitfire Le Mans engines, complete with its cast-iron eight port cylinder head and large Weber carburettors, but not yet with the strut supports between carburettors and cylinder block to eliminate vibration*

BELOW LEFT: Dramatis personae *at Le Mans, on the pit counter, in 1964—(left to right) Rob Slotemaker, John Lloyd, Roger Sykes (mechanic), David Hobbs, Lyndon Mills and Fred Nicklin*

BELOW: *Peter Bolton (in helmet), John Lloyd (centre) and Rob Slotemaker worrying over a point in Le Mans car preparation, 1964*

Spitfires (there was no way, he once insisted to me, that his cars would carry completely non-standard body styles such as those used on the works Sprites of the period). Fortunately, the Spitfire GT prototype had been returned to Coventry by the end of 1963, complete with its steel fastback hatchback by Michelotti, so it was decided to make fibreglass derivatives of that roof style for the new race cars. These were made, quite literally, by laying up the

fibreglass mat on the Spitfire GT prototype itself— by using one car as the mould for another.

I ought to repeat, yet again, that the GT6 did not develop from the shape of the racing Spitfires, but that the racing cars developed from the prototype GT6. The problem is that Standard-Triumph's own advertising agents confused the issue to make the arrival of the GT6 more dramatic, and said this, 'New Triumph GT6, born in Le Mans. . . If you were at Le Mans last year the new GT6 may look familiar. It is bred from the works Triumph Spitfires that came first and second in their class. . . .' To tell the truth, however, would have spoilt a rather romantic story.

The shape, incidentally, certainly proved itself to be efficient but as far as I know (and I was intimately concerned with the project) its performance was never checked in a wind tunnel. In the same way, the faired-in headlamps were no more and no less than neat copies of the Jaguar E type installation, and were assumed to be aerodynamically more efficient than the standard exposed layout.

LEFT: *All four Le Mans cars—ADU1B, ADU2B, ADU3B, and ADU4B—ready to leave for France. The fourth car was not used at all during the weekend, but the three numbered cars all raced*

BELOW LEFT: *The three Spitfires lined up at the pits before the start of the 1964 24-Hour race. The car which finished was No. 50 (ADU2B)*

BELOW: *Similar to the Stage II layout, but* not *the same, the Le Mans Spitfire installation of April 1964*

The first two Le Mans Spitfires to be built (and taken to the Le Mans test weekend in April 1964) were equipped with normal production-car bonnets, fashioned in light alloy because time had run out by the time they had to be sent to France; as I recall, the bonnets were actually 'borrowed' from the rallying department. Later, in 1965, attempts were made to improve the aerodynamics even further by 'spatting' the rear wheel arches, but these were never raced. It was, in any case, the wrong end at which to look for improvement, as the noses, which were hung about with extra lamps, and with quick-lift jacking brackets, were not at all smoothly profiled.

The three competing Spitfires at Le Mans in 1964. Note the tiny radiator air intakes, the circular air intake connected to trunking to the cockpit, and the extra wheel arch flaring

Reducing the weight was tackled in two ways. Apart from the fact that all unnecessary trim could be discarded, the homologated rally cars could have light-alloy body skin panels (the regulations mentioned that the material of any panel 'licked by the air stream' could be changed) instead of steel, and Perspex side and rear windows in place of glass, plus different seats. The Le Mans cars, being 'prototypes' could change anything, so every main panel on the car was made out of light alloy.

This was very difficult to achieve in the time, for it was necessary to schedule a short run of light-alloy pressings at the end of a normal steel panel pressings batch at Forward Radiator. Since alloy panels really require different clearances between the two halves of a press die, it meant that considerable quantities of 'scrap' panels were produced in some haste. It was a procedure, spread over many weeks, which the production engineers were not anxious to have to repeat.

Improving the braking was straightforward enough, for considerably larger Girling front discs and rear drums could be fixed to existing suspension pick-up points without altering anything, or even without breaking (or even bending) the regulations. Getting the roadholding right, on the other hand, was a different matter.

Whatever might have been desired, it was not possible to change the basic geometry—on the rally cars because the regulations forbade it, and on the race cars because Harry Webster wanted the world to see near-standard cars being used. Fred Nicklin, Standard-Triumph's chief tester (who later owned the much-modified version of one of the rally Spitfires), spent ages trying to produce a stable system. He wasn't helped by a limitation on wheel rim widths (4.5 in. rims were eventually homologated, as were bolt-on light-alloy wheels), nor by the fact that it was desirable to raise the nose of the rally cars to give more ground clearance. Tuning the

front suspension was easy, but sorting out the swing axle rear was not. For a sprint car, with one driver and negligible fuel loads the solution was obvious; to cater for two-up, and up to 18 gallons of fuel with the Le Mans tank, was more difficult. The eventual compromise, to provide a much stiffer spring, consistent and constant negative camber, and very sturdy dampers, seemed to work quite well.

Right from the start (and remembering Harry Webster's experience with the TRS) it was decided to split the operation in half. Four Le Mans Spitfires were to be built from scratch in the main experimental shop—by John Lloyd's office—while five

ADU3B, driven by Jean-Francois Piot at this point, in the 1964 Le Mans race. Later it crashed, when its driver (Jean-Louis Marnat) became asphyxiated by an entry of exhaust fumes)

rally Spitfires would be prepared from production-build cars delivered from Canley in the spring of 1964, in the competitions department at the back of the engineering building. In the meantime, one test car—412VC, the original Spitfire used for publicity pictures in 1962—could be used in British rallies to shake the bugs out of the components and prove the

philosophy of the changes. Ray Henderson was to be the chief mechanic over both programmes, while the author left the Le Mans project to John Lloyd and Lyndon Mills.

At first there was no mistaking a race car for a rally car, for race cars had special bonnets with faired-in headlamps, GT6-style fastback coupé tops, and were painted dark green, while rally cars had normal Spitfire profiles, and were painted powder blue (as the TR4s had been in 1962 and 1963). From September 1964, however, things got more confusing, for the team rally cars (except for one—ADU8B—which was always the test/practice/spare in 1964 and 1965, and never actually started an event) were treated to modified versions of the fastback hardtop, and for the Tour de France only they actually borrowed Le Mans car bonnets, repainted for the occasion.

The race cars, complete (in 1964) with TR4 gearboxes, letter-box slots in their driver's door windows, and other unique racing features, were registered ADU1B, 2B, 3B and 4B, and carried Experimental Department chassis numbers X727, X728, X730 and X731 respectively.

LEFT: *In preparation for the 1965 Le Mans race, Triumph tested cars with aerodynamic differences which in this case included Perspex 'fences' across the bonnet, and part-enclosing rear wheel spats. The spats were not used in the race. Bill Bradley is driving this car, at Silverstone*

BELOW LEFT: *The rebuilt ADU3B at Le Mans in 1965, complete with 'bug-deflector' across its bonnet. It was driven by Claude Dubois and Jean-Francois Piot, and took second place in its class behind the Thuner/Lampinen Spitfire*

BELOW: *Pitwork on ADU3B at Le Mans 1965, showing the final method of supplying cold air to the air intakes of the Weber carburettors*

The rally programme was immediately complicated by a deal cooked up between Standard-Triumph BP (who provided the team's lubricants and fuel), and Stirling Moss, whereby a rally Spitfire would be prepared for Stirling's secretary Valerie Pirie to drive in SMART (Stirling Moss Automobile Racing Team) colours of rather bilious (nicknamed at the time as vomit) green, whenever and wherever the full factory team was entered in 1964–5. The four powder blue team cars, therefore, were ADU5B, 6B, 7B and 8B (with 8B being nominated as the spare car until or unless one of the other three machines was crashed), while the SMART car was ADU 467B. The SMART car differed in that it was never treated to the GT6-style fastback, though it followed suit in all other respects.

To complete the team car chronology, when the Finn Simo Lampinen, joined the team for 1965, he insisted on a left-hand-drive car. All other team cars had right-hand-drive, so a new car was prepared and registered AVC654B for the 1965 season. This did not replace any other car, but was added to the team, and became the sixth and last rally car to be prepared.

To avoid confusion, it will be best now to divide the description purely into race car, and rally car, activities, with suitable cross reference where appropriate.

RIGHT: *The Macau car, with a very lightweight body, being assembled in August 1965. Note the gutted doors, the very basic instrument panel, and the wrap-around 'single-seater' windscreen*

BELOW RIGHT: *Rear view of the Macau Spitfire, made from available parts after the 1965 Le Mans effort had been completed*

BELOW: *The 'Macau' Spitfire, built up (so it is claimed) from spare parts in the summer of 1965, and shipped out to ZF Garages of Hong Kong for Walter Sulke to race*

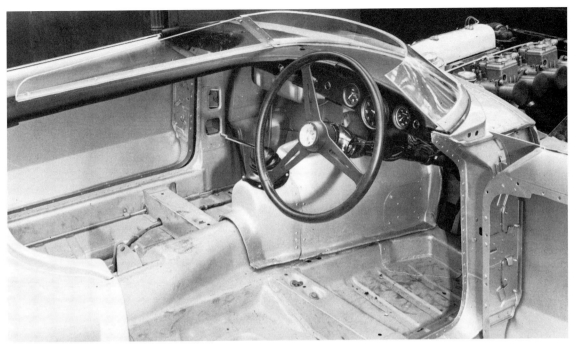

Racing Spitfires—1964 to 1966

Construction of all four Le Mans cars began early in 1964, by which time engine testing was well under way, and component supplies were flooding in. The 70X project took up a great deal of the engineering department's time (anyone not believing why firms withdraw from racing 'to get on with production car development', should have been at Standard-Triumph in 1964!) especially as no fewer than 15 engines were ordered for racing, rallying, or test and development purposes. It is interesting to note that the final-drive ratio for the Le Mans race was initially to have been 4.11:1, which would certainly have been too low (it was changed to a 3.89:1 ratio at a very early stage), and that the use of a limited-slip differential was not even considered until January 1964. It is a measure of the factory's commitment, and their 'pull' with suppliers, that adequate supplies of a specially-designed small Salisbury differential unit were built in time for the April test weekend.

There was a huge amount of development work needed to make the 1147 cc engines reliable, powerful, and race-ready, and one test bed was virtually allocated full-time to the process. Work centred on optimising the cylinder head, breathing, and valve gear, and on making all the working clearances right, while making sure that oil pressure could be retained, and that head gaskets stayed sealed. It was not until the beginning of June 1964, just before Le Mans, that the job was done.

Although it helped considerably that a new eight-port cylinder head was already in existence for future production cars, this did not prove capable of

In the winter of 1965/66, one prototype of the six-cylinder GT6R project was started, but never finished

breathing deeply enough and new heads had to be designed. For the race cars, a cast-iron cylinder head was chosen, having an 11.75:1 compression ratio, 42DCOE Weber twin-choke carburettors with 38 mm chokes, and a camshaft which used 104 degrees of overlap. The valves were so large that there was no space for conventional spark plugs, and 10 mm (motorcycle-type) racing plugs had to be used instead. Testbed reference engines produced 98 bhp (net) at 6750 rpm, with peak torque of 84 lb. ft at 5000 rpm. By comparison, the aluminium cylinder head used on rally cars produced 102.5 bhp at 7000 rpm, and peak torque of 86 lb. ft at 5500 rpm—but the unit was not, at the time, thought to be reliable enough for full-power use over a 24-hour period.

The first car to be finished was tested at Oulton Park by racing drivers Peter Bolton and David Hobbs, along with tester Fred Nicklin, early in April 1964, when it lost all its oil pressure after a 65-lap shake-down session. A few days later, however, this

and another car completed many laps at the Le Mans practice weekend. Both cars lapped in around 4 min. 55 sec., and were timed at 130 mph on the Mulsanne Straight; neither, incidentally had the faired-headlamp bonnet at this stage.

For the Le Mans race itself, only two firm entries had been accepted, along with one reserve, but four new cars were taken along on a massive transporter, and the third entry was accepted during the course of practice. The team's line-up was as follows:

ADU 1B Comp. no. 49 (Mike Rothschild/Bob Tullius)

The part-built GT6R prototype, intended for Le Mans, which was abandoned at the start of 1966. The six cylinder engine, at this stage, was a developed version of that used in Triumph 2000 rally cars, which explains the use of cast-iron exhaust manifolds

ADU2B Comp. no. 50 (David Hobbs/Rob Slote-
maker)
ADU3B Comp. no. 65 (Jean-Louis Marnat/Jean-
Francois Piot)
ADU4B was present, but did not practice, or
race.

It was an event which might have been, but
fortunately was not, tragic for Standard-Triumph,
for two of the cars were eliminated in crashes.
Mercifully, neither driver was seriously or lastingly
injured. It had been a routine start, with the
Spitfires lapping in less than five minutes, and
achieving up to 134 mph on the straights (so that E
type bonnet shape *was* worth it, after all). After two
hours, however, Mike Rothschild crashed ADU1B
heavily under the Dunlop Bridge, just after the pits.
Perhaps Rothschild simply overcooked it, and
perhaps he was pushed off line by a faster car—but
the result was that the car was wrecked.

*Peter Cox, a Standard-Triumph racing mechanic, bought the ex-
SMART rally car (ADU467B) after the department had
closed down, and raced it in Britain with great success*

Later, at 04.30 am, more than 12 hours into the
race, Jean-Louis Marnat crashed ADU3B just
beyond the pits, at rather low speed, and it was
conclusively established that this was due to him
becoming gassed by exhaust fumes in the cockpit let
in through the tail damaged by an earlier in-
discretion at Tertre Rouge. Like its sister car,
ADU3B was seriously damaged.

The third car, however, driven by David Hobbs
and Rob Slotemaker, finished strongly in 21st place,
averaging 94.7 mph including all stops, and record-
ing the remarkable fuel consumption of 22.4 mpg.
The car finished third in its capacity class behind
two Alpine-Renaults. However, it beat the works
Austin-Healey Sprite of Clive Baker and Bill
Bradley convincingly—by no less than 124 miles, or
5.2 mph average over the full 24 hours, and this was
in spite of the fact that the Sprite had a very non-
standard body and was a lot lighter. The three
Spitfires, incidentally, weighed in at 1640 lb.,
1635 lb., and 1625 lb. respectively—the minor
differences being attributable to the different fuel
loads being carried at scrutineering.

It was the only race tackled by the Spitfires in
1964, and the next few months were divided
between attention to the rallying programme, to the

building up of two new cars to replace the crashed Le Mans cars, and to further development. One major discussion point among the engineers was about lightening the standard chassis frame. Tests had been carried out by the rig test department before the start of the 1964 programme to see if the drilling of holes or the cutting out of sections would be acceptable. The biggest weight saving on the bare frame (normally weighing 102.5 lb.) was a mere 15 lb., but there was such a loss in torsional rigidity that the idea was abandoned. At the end of 1964, however, another approach was tried. A complete frame was built up of normal-shape and profile pressings, but in 20 SWG instead of 18 SWG thickness. This resulted in a 31 lb. weight saving, and although the loss of rigidity was still considerable it was decided that it should be built up into a car for test. The result was that the Le Mans cars for 1965 (but not the Sebring cars) were fitted with the lightened frame, and no-one complained too much about a loss of handling precision. The weight problem had struck home, for in the 1964 race the Sprite had weighed 1455 lb., and the class-winning Alpine-Renaults about 1450 lb. each.

In the meantime, pressure from North America (and a certain amount of financial help from the importers) persuaded the factory to prepare a team for the Sebring 12-Hour race in March 1965. All four factory race cars were sent out to Florida, where ADU 1B/2B/4B were driven by Bolton/Rothschild, Tullius/Gates and Barker/Feuerhelm respectively.

In this event they ran as homologated Grand Touring cars, as did the Dick Jacobs special-bodied MG Midget, driven by Andrew Hedges and Roger Mac. This was the only occasion on which a Spridget beat the Spitfire, for the Midget won the class, from Barker/Feuerhelm and Tullius/Gates respectively; the other Spitfire had to be retired after Peter Bolton rolled it over—this was ADU 1B, which had to be extensively rebuilt before Le Mans in June. The fact that they finally ran as GT cars explains why a winter proposal to run non-homologated 5.5 in. alloy wheel rims at the rear had to be abandoned.

Apart from the team rally cars, there was a semi-works car in 1964–5 for Valerie Pirie, Stirling Moss's secretary. This is a posed picture, in a press car, taken outside Stirling's West End house

The question of which car was which—registration or chassis numbers notwithstanding—began to get rather difficult to monitor in 1965, as it always does in an active competitions workshop. Not only had two new team cars been built up to replace the original written-off ADU1B and ADU3B, but a fifth car was also assembled and (from May 1965) was put out on more-or-less permanent loan to Bill Bradley. This was ERW412C, and I have not treated it as a true team car, though it was identical in almost every respect—I cover its fortunes later in this narrative. In addition the bare bones of a sixth car also took shape, though this car was not completed for the time being. It was, by any standards, a very costly programme. John Lloyd recently confirmed that Le Mans in 1964 had cost about £110,000 (which included the cost of building the cars in the first place); in 1965 this figure rose even further.

The reason was simple—that in 1965 entries were put in for four cars, on the assumption that there was no way that all four would be accepted. It came as a rigid shock to the team (still actively controlled by Harry Webster, with John Lloyd and Lyndon Mills as his deputies) when they all were. There were two problems—not only was it going to cost a lot more, but it was also going to stretch the resources of the mechanics to the limit.

RIGHT: *Terry Hunter and Patrick Lier missed a* Coupe des Alpes *by one minute in the 1964 Alpine Rally. It was also the only time that the team Spitfires were used with standard 'bubble-top' hardtops*

BELOW: *The first four team rally cars being prepared in the spring of 1964. Though originally built on the Canley assembly lines, their bodies were immediately separated from the backbone frames. There are five frames but only four bodies in this shot . . .*

For Le Mans in 1965 a thorough pre-event development programme was carried out, both to lighten the cars, and to try to give them even more straight speed. On the event the cars looked identical to the 1964 race cars except that they carried extra fog lamps on each side of the grille, though rear wheelarch spats had been tried in testing. Lightening was achieved by fitting the thin-section chassis frames, the light-alloy cylinders heads (now pronounced race-ready), small rear brake drums (8 in. Vitesse type instead of 9 in. TR4 type), and GT6-type all-synchromesh gearboxes. They were also entered as homologated GT cars, as at Sebring. The factory claimed that more than 100 lb. had been saved—and this was borne out at

Ready to leave for the Tour de France 1964—the team rally cars, equipped for the first time with the Le Mans-style hardtops, and with a borrowed set of faired-headlamp bonnets from the Le Mans cars themselves

scrutineering, where the 'official' pre-race weights were all around 1520 lb.

The cars to start were as follows;

ADU1B Comp. no. 52 (David Hobbs/Rob
                     Slotemaker)
ADU2B Comp. no. 53 (Bill Bradley/Peter Bolton)
ADU3B Comp. no. 54 (Claude Dubois/Jean-
                     Francois Piot)
ADU4B Comp. no. 60 (Jean-Jacques
                     Thuner/Simo Lampinen)

The last car, the reserve in the original plan, was driven by two of the rally team. The Alpine Rally (which usually clashed with Le Mans) was several weeks later in the season in 1965.

Compared with 1964, it was an even more successful outing, for ADU4B finished 13th overall and won its capacity class, at 95.1 mph, while ADU3B finished 14th, not far behind it. ADU2B retired with a blown engine after the front mounted oil cooler split, while ADU1B was eliminated when

Rob Slotemaker obligingly pulled over to allow a faster car to pass him during the night, dipped his lights, and failed to get round the next corner! Harry Webster was not impressed!

On this occasion, let me make it clear, an Austin-Healey Sprite (driven by Paul Hawkins and John Rhodes) finished 12th, 32 miles and 1.2 mph ahead, but as this car had an entirely non-standard body, a five-speed gearbox and a Mini-Cooper S 1293 cc engine it couldn't be counted as a production car and ran as a Prototype.

Part of the reason for the greater speed in 1965 was that the 1147 cc. engines had been made even more powerful, by the use of 45DCOE carburettors, and produced 109 bhp at 7300 rpm with the aid of a 120 degree overlap camshaft. In top speed the 1965 cars could nudge 140 mph, and this could probably have been improved upon if time had been available to clean up the nose to any extent.

Soon after they returned from Le Mans, the three undamaged race cars (ADU2B, ADU3B, and ADU4B) were loaned to a team of drivers which

included Roy Fidler, to drive at Silverstone in the 750MC's 6-hour relay. It was all very good publicity, and great fun, but the cars were not really suited to such a tight little circuit (the club circuit was used) and no prizes were gained.

And that, in fact, was almost the end of the racing Spitfires' works careers, though there are several other events to be mentioned. During the summer, one keen amateur racing driver from Hong Kong, the Standard-Triumph importer Walter Sulke of ZF Garages, persuaded Harry Webster to build up a special Spitfire 'sprint' car for him to race at the Macau GP and other events in the Far East. Both John Lloyd and Ray Henderson have said that this car was really built up 'from a box of spare parts',

Tour de France 1964 service halt, with everything in order. This is Jean-Jacques Thuner's car (ADU5B). Thuner is standing by the car. Behind it (left to right) are Rob Slotemaker, John Gretener (Thuner's co-driver) and the author

but it seems fair to assume that it was built around the bare bones of the unfinished sixth car mentioned already, and converted into a smart open 'single-seater', with a headrest behind the driver, a Perspex wrap-around racing screen and with a rigid cover over the empty passenger seat. Details of the construction are told better in pictures than in words, and several illustrations of the building of the car are included in these pages. It raced at Macau on 27–28 November 1965, with some success, then won several other events in the region, before eventually being sold to North America. Its last sighting, in very non-standard form, was in California.

Before this, Bill Bradley, who first drove for the team in the 1964 Tour de France, had persuaded Harry Webster to lend him a spare race car for the 1965 season, this being effectively 'No. 5', and

registered ERW412C. Its first event was in the Nürburgring 1000 km race in West Germany, in May 1965, when it broke a drive shaft while leading the works MG Midget, but it went on to set several new lap records in British and Irish club races, and won outright at Pheonix Park, Dublin, Brands Hatch, and Castle Combe.

By the end of 1965, however, this car effectively lost its separate identity, as the factory had withdrawn from racing, and whenever Bradley's car was crashed, or needed new major components, they were robbed from another car. The 1966 car, carrying ADU2B, however, was very special, as Bradley once suggested to me in a letter,

'During the latter part of 1965 quite a lot of testing was done, and during the winter of 1965–6 Standard-Triumph agreed to run a special Spitfire for the 1966 season. A lengthy list of modifications was ... agreed to by Harry Webster. This resulted in easily the fastest and best handling Triumph Spitfire that was ever produced.'

It was unbeatable in its class at first but at the Nürburgring 1000 km race it collided with the race leader when leading both works Sprites by several minutes, and the replacement car was never quite as rapid. The secret of the car, incidentally, was a Lotus Elan-like strut-type independent rear suspension, which was under consideration for another racing project, and in 1966 the result was that

---

RIGHT: *Who says that swing-axle cars can't be made to handle? That is Rob Slotemaker's class-winning Spitfire in the 1964 Tour de France, cornering at very high speed!*

BELOW: *Tour de France 1964, all lined up for the one hour race at Rouen, with Slotemaker's Spitfire on the front row alongside the works MGB, and Cheinisse's works Alpine-Renault. Thuner's car is on the second row, with another of the Alpine-Renault team*

Bradley won 14 classes out of 18 starts, and only retired once—in the Nürburgring crash. At the end of the season it held class lap records at Goodwood, Brands Hatch, Crystal Palace, Snetterton, Oulton Park and Mallory Park.

Although the factory withdrew from racing towards the end of 1965 (because new homologation regulations were about to outlaw the lightweight Spitfires), they did seriously consider entering special developed prototype GT6s (to be called GT6Rs) for the 1966 Le Mans race. One of the surviving four-cylinder cars—which must, by definition, have been ADU3B or ADU4B (though no documentation exists to tell us which)—was considerably modified during the winter of 1965–6,

---

ADU6B and ADU7B about to leave for the 1964 Geneva rally, in which 7B (driven by Terry Hunter) took second overall, the 6B (Thuner) was fifth. Interesting detail shows the 'luggage-loading' slot in the fibreglass hardtop, which was unique to rally cars, and the panel covering the 18-gallon fuel tanks which filled the space behind the seats and ahead of the stowage space. Normal-shape bonnets were fitted

to include strut-type rear suspension, and a 1998 cc GT6 engine equipped with three twin-choke Weber carburettors. Although fuel injection (by Lucas) had already briefly been tested on one of the Le Mans cars, but never practiced or raced, and even though Bill Bradley would be racing a Triumph 2000 in the British Saloon Car Championship of 1966, injection was not tried on the GT6R at this point. Up to 175 bhp was confidently expected (the 1964–5 rallying 2000 saloons with Weber carburettors produced about 150 bhp), and this might have resulted in a top speed of more than 160 mph. By early 1966, however, the competitions programme was rapidly being run down, and the project was abandoned. The car was subsequently dismantled.

Was it all worth it? Could a cost approaching £150,000 for the successful 1965 Le Mans programme be justified? Harry Webster and John Carpenter are both convinced that it was, while John Lloyd is sure that much of the engineering experience was valuable to future production Spitfires and GT6s. All, however, feel that the company might have tried even harder, in marketing terms, to capitalize on the programme.

Rallying Spitfires—1964 and 1965

Unlike the race cars, the 'team' rally Spitfires were not built from scratch, but were based on a set of five powder blue hardtop Spitfires delivered, as new, from the Canley production lines in February–March 1964. Four of these were proper works cars and kept their powder blue paint throughout their works careers; the fifth, for Val Pirie and the Stirling Moss team, was always maintained in the factory competitions department, but was re-painted in that characteristic green chosen by Moss for his cars at this period.

Because these cars had to be homologated, some of the non-standard items fitted to the race cars could not be used. Neither was it possible to give the rally cars the same leisurely preparation treatment as the race cars received, for a much more intensive programme of events was planned. Although the Moss-Pirie-Spitfire partnership only lasted for twelve months (and ended after the Tulip Rally of 1965), the team cars competed in nine different events before the end of 1965, not all of which had been planned in the first place!

In time for the first event in the programme, the Alpine Rally of June 1964, four cars (ADU 5B, 6B, 7B, and 467B which was the SMART car) were equipped with aluminium body skin panels, aluminium-head versions of the 70X Le Mans engines, gearboxes with Vitesse ratios, 4.5 in. rim width steel disc wheels (from the Courier van) larger front disc calipers, 8 in. Vitesse rear brake drums, 4.55 : 1 final drive ratios with a limited slip differentials, oil coolers, special seats, extra lamps, and many other details. Visually they looked almost standard, except that the bumpers had been removed, and extra lamps fitted at front and rear.

In the meantime ADU 8B had been completed first of all, and used for recconnaisance (it was, incidentally, crashed heavily by Terry Hunter on its

The 1965 team rally cars had this type of fascia—a modified version of the standard layout. This was a Monte Carlo Rally car, with a heated front screen

way back through France after the event)—a role for which it was preserved for the next two seasons. The original development car, the prototype, 412VC, in which Roy Fidler had taken second overall position in the Welsh International Rally, was sold off to Terry Hunter for his private use.

For the Alpine the cars were driven by,

ADU5B by Jean-Jacques Thuner/John Gretener,
ADU6B by Roy Fidler/Don Grimshaw,
ADU7B by Terry Hunter/Patrick Lier
—and—
ADU467B by Valerie Pirie/Yvonne Hilton.

It was immediately obvious, not only that the very highly-tuned cars were real pigs to start from cold (I lost count of the number of times a push start was needed), but that mountain motoring could be real misery with a non-synchronised first gear. The biggest misery of all, though, was the fact that BMC were able to enter extensively modified 1275 Mini-Cooper S saloons in the same class as the Spitfires, and often did. In the Alpine they sent Rauno Aaltonen out to tackle not only the Spitfires but the entire GT category.

The Spitfires made a good, but not sensational start. Fidler's car melted a piston (this often happened to these cars, right to the end of their

careers—it proved just how close to the razor-edge the tune actually was), while Thuner's car was eliminated in a crash with a non-competing car. Valerie Pirie's car went off the road, and had to be retrieved with the aid of a breakdown truck. Hunter's car lost a single minute on a road section (which was my fault, not his, for in practice we had under-estimated the amount by which the organizers would 'prune' one of the tightest road sections), and therefore missed a Coupe des Alpes. As a result he finished third in the 1.3-litre class, which was won by Aaltonen's 'GT' Mini-Cooper S, which was unpenalised on the road.

A post-mortem, held back in the factory during July, chaired by Harry Webster, led to the conclusion that there was nothing to be done about the poor cold starting, or lack of low-speed torque without de-tuning the engines (and, therefore, making the cars slower), but it was decided that the cars should henceforth be fitted with prototype all-synchromesh GT6 gearboxes. This, though strictly illegal in sporting terms, did not make the cars any faster, but it certainly spared the transmissions in the future.

For the Tour de France, therefore, to be held in September, it was decided to use the same four cars, but to make several major changes to suit the requirements of a 10-day event which not only included speed hillclimb tests and special stages, but which included hour-long circuit races at places like Rheims, Le Mans, Rouen and Monza.

To ensure adequate fuel range the light-alloy 18-gallon fuel tanks as used on race cars were installed in the car (much of the extra capacity being

The Monte Carlo rally Spitfires, ready to start from London, and to be driven by Terry Hunter (7B), Rob Slotemaker (6B) and Simo Lampinen (654B). This was the first time that the special 'four-headlamp' bonnets had been used

accomodated immediately behind the seats, down into the floor area), and to ensure a high top speed a different version of the race car fastback body was grafted on in fibreglass (for rally car use it incorporated an opening slot in the tail to allow a spare wheel to be extracted); at the same time the team 'borrowed' the race car faired-headlamp bonnets, and painted them powder blue for the occasion. It was the only time these bonnets were used on the rally cars by the factory team. The Le Mans car engines with cast-iron heads were used, along with the 3.89:1 final drive ratios, and with the all-synchromesh gearboxes installed. Cast-alloy road wheels of Le Mans type were also used on the circuits, and sometimes on the road, but supplies of steel wheels were also carried for road use with road tyres.

The only driver changes were made essential by the regulations (which stated that a co-driver had to drive some of the tests himself), so racing drivers Bill Bradley and Rob Slotemaker joined Roy Fidler and Terry Hunter in 6B and 7B respectively, while Susan Reeves joined Val Pirie in 467B which, incidentally, ran with the faired-bonnet but retained its normal bubble hardtop.

Even though three out of the four cars retired— all with serious engine problems—it was still a triumph for Triumph. Bradley's car melted a piston at Rheims, the first event, where the SMART car also threw a connecting rod, and Thuner's car also melted a piston near the end of the event. The Slotemaker/Hunter can (ADU7B), however, soundly beat every works or semi-works Alpine-Renault and Bonnet (Renault) in the 1.3-litre GT

class. In spite of the fact that at one point it ran out of petrol (on a road section, miles from service help), and that for the last two days the fuel tank was leaking into the cockpit, the team won their class, finished fifth in the GT handicap category, and 10th on scratch. Triumph's French importers originally couldn't believe it, and were then ecstatic, while Alpine-Renault were devastated, to put it mildly.

Immediately after this there was a scramble to re-prepare the team cars for unscheduled events. Thuner's 5B was re-engined, but not brought home, and loaned to the French importers for Jean-Francois Piot and Jean-Louis Marnat to race in the Paris 1000 km race at Montlhéry, where it averaged 77.05 mph, never missed a beat, and won its GT capacity class.

6B and 7B, however, were rushed back to the factory, re-prepared with normal-shape bonnets and a change of gearing, before being sent out to Switzerland to compete in the Geneva Rally, driven by Thuner and Hunter respectively. It was an event ideally suited to the Spitfires, for it carried a class-by-class handicap marking system, and the result was that Terry Hunter finished second overall behind the winning 4.7-litre Ford Falcon of Henri Greder, Thuner finished fifth, the cars took first and second in their class, *and* won the team prize with the

Rob Slotemaker and Alan Taylor on their way through Northern France on the way to second in class in the 1965 Monte Carlo Rally

help of a privately-entered Spitfire from Switzerland.

Valerie Pirie's SMART car had not been involved in the Geneva, but she then entered her car for the RAC Rally of that year, even though it was not really suitable; the team's drivers, incidentally, were entered in Triumph 2000s. Predictably enough, the Spitfire succumbed to the battering of the rough forestry tracks, and didn't finish; Roy Fidler's Triumph 2000 took sixth place overall.

For 1965, and to take advantage of the new single-filament quartz-halogen headlamp bulbs which were just becoming available, it was decided to fit auxiliary double-dipping headlamps inboard of the usual position, in neat streamlined pods. (This feature had also been adopted for BMC's Big Healeys, and was not a true innovation.) The major change for 1965, however, was that the brilliant young Finn, Simo Lampinen, joined the team, as did Rob Slotemaker. For a time, at least, Triumph had too many drivers. At Lampinen's insistence a left-hand-drive Spitfire (registered AVC654B) was assembled, becoming the sixth and last works Spitfire to be built.

The Monte Carlo Rally was run in appalling blizzard conditions throughout. There were three team cars (6B for Slotemaker, 7B for Hunter, 654B for Lampinen), Pirie in the SMART car, and Thuner in his own Spitfire with a works-loaned engine and transmission. During the event Hunter crashed his car, and Pirie ran out of time. Lampinen actually arrived in Monaco in tenth place overall, with Slotemaker not far behind.

On the final run, Slotemaker rose to finish 14th, and second in the class to Timo Makinen (whose Mini-Cooper S won the event outright), while both Lampinen's and Thuner's cars blew their engines. Terry Hunter, incidentally, blotted his copybook by trying to get on to the special stages on the last night, ostensibly to help his colleagues, lost his competition licence as a result, and left the team (and rallying) forthwith.

Three further events were tackled by the team cars in 1965. In the Tulip Rally, only Lampinen and Valerie Pirie had Spitfires, when Lampinen's car over-cooked its clutch at the start of a speed hillclimb, and Ms. Pirie managed to finish, but without winning any awards. In June, in the Geneva Rally, 5B was entered for Thuner, and 654B for Lampinen, the result being that Thuner took fifth overall in the event, and second overall in the entire GT category (to an Alfa Romeo GTZ Tubolare), with a class win into the bargain.

Valerie Pirie's last event in the Spitfire—the 1965 Tulip Rally. Her co-driver was Susan Reeves

Lampinen was second in that class.

The Alpine Rally of 1965 was a splendid final fling. It was the last event programmed for the cars (there was no Tour de France held in 1965) and as there was a separate category for Prototypes Triumph decided to make their Spitfires even more special than usual. To the normal rallying specification they added the use of larger (1964 Le Mans-type) braking systems, and they also fitted prototype 1296 cc engines.

The enlarged engines, in fact, were due to be revealed in a quantity-production Triumph saloon—the front-wheel-drive 1300—later in the year, and plenty of cylinder blocks were already available. A study of the 'pass-off' power curves produced for the Alpine Rally engines shows a peak power of 117 bhp at 7000 rpm, and peak torque of 97 lb. ft at 5500 rpm. Not only was there more torque throughout the range, however, but it was a much smoother delivery than ever before, and the cars were rather easier to drive. The previous best figure for an 1147 cc engine had been 109 bhp at 7300 rpm, and this had been with more extreme camshaft timing.

The usual four cars were entered—5B, 6B, 7B and 654B for Thuner, Fidler, Slotemaker and Lampinen respectively—on what was certainly the fastest schedule Alpine Rally ever held until then. Other 'prototypes' in the category included Matra-

Bonnets and Porsche 904, one driven by Mercedes-Benz team driver Eugen Böhringer. The author occupied the co-driver's seat of one of the cars, alongside Roy Fidler.

The result was sensational. Two cars retired—Fidler's 6B with broken rear wheel studs, and Slotemaker's 7B with other mechanical problems—but Lampinen's car went on to win the Prototype category *outright*, with Thuner's car second overall, right behind him. All the semi-racing cars originally pitted against the Spitfires were either out-paced, or were eliminated.

In their issue of 3 December 1965, *Autocar* published driving impressions, and full performance figures, of ADU6B, which had been re-fitted with an 1147 cc engine but was otherwise in Alpine Rally form. The results were remarkable. The car was geared right down (with a 4.55:1 final drive ratio), and was limited to 105 mph at 7000 rpm in top gear, and it also recorded the abysmal fuel consumption of 15.3 mpg, but it also sprinted to the quarter mile in 17.8 sec., to 60 mph in 10.3 sec, and to 100 mph in 33.9 sec.

Fine profile, fine rally car. This was one of the 'prototype' 1296 cc engined cars on their way to a Category win in the 1965 Alpine rally, way up on the heights of Mont Ventoux

Postscript

When the decision to wind down all competition activity came in February 1966, most of the Spitfires left the factory, though complete records are not available. As far as I can see, ADU1B was never rebuilt after its Le Mans crash, ADU2B was raced by Bill Bradley until he crashed it, and ADU3B or 4B was the part-complete GT6R. Bradley's programme, in Ray Henderson's words, 'gradually used up' the other race cars, and the rest of the parts had gone into making the open car sent out to Hong Kong at the end of 1965.

The fate of *all* the rally cars is less clear. AVC654B, the left-hand-drive car, was sold to the Swedish Triumph importers, while race/rally mechanics Peter Cox and Chris Williams bought ADU467B and ADU8B respectively. A complicated series of events led to ADU7B being rebuilt around a new chassis frame with strut-type independent rear suspension, for Bill Bradley to race,

and an even more complicated sequence led to factory tester Fred Nicklin buying the much modified bodyshell, a standard chassis, and a 70X racing engine for his own use, but without the distinctive registration number. In 1981, this car was bought by Peter Donnelly, and regained its famous registration number. Of ADU5B and ADU6B I have no news, though I was told not too long ago that one perfectly authentic Spitfire rally car had found its way into the private collection in the Midlands. . . . ADU8B, incidentally, was eventually sold to Japan.

Cox, Williams, and Peter Clarke (another mechanic from the Coventry competitions department) eventually got together in racing their ex-works

The definitive Spitfire team rally car, as tested by Autocar *in December 1965. This was the most successful individual car (ADU7B), parts of which still survive in a rebodied car*

Spitfires and indirectly helped to cause the run-down of special fibreglass and light-alloy stocks. As Ray Henderson once told me, every time they crashed a car, or needed new parts, they came back to the factory and bought more parts—'they just seemed to keep on building Spitfires'—which explains how ADU8B came to have a fastback body (which it most assuredly never had in true works hands), and how it had such a hybrid specification when used in Classic Car racing in the mid-1970s. Their cars were very successful in British club and marque racing, and for a time the Gold Seal Car Co. of South London became involved. In 1967, in the ex-SMART car, Peter Cox won the Freddie Dixon

Trophy, and later he prepared the Gold Seal Spitfires used by Richard Lloyd and Chris Marshall. For 1970 he even managed to evolve a one-off racing GT6, built up around a standard chassis and suspension in Mk 2 (lower-wishbone rear suspension) form, but with the GT6R type of 175 bhp engine, and most of the remaining stock of light alloy and fibreglass body panels in his own workshops.

Simo Lampinen, with Harry Webster, signing to drive in 1965

Chapter 5
In the family: GT6 cocktail

Although the design of a six-cylinder derivative of the Spitfire was not seriously considered until the Spitfire itself had been on sale for 18 months, such a car had always been a feasible proposition. It needed no more than a glance at the four-cylinder Herald and six-cylinder Vitesse, allied to a bit of wishful thinking, to confirm that.

A superficial thumbnail sketch of the GT6 would describe it as a fastback version of the Spitfire with a more powerful version of the six-cylinder Vitesse engine shoehorned in to the engine bay, but the evolution of the car was much more complicated than that. It was quite true, however, that the layout of the Vitesse was a very important factor, and the description of GT6 origins must therefore begin there.

Every Standard-Triumph car of the 1940s and 1950s was fitted with a four-cylinder engine. It was not until the great expansion of the 1950s got under way (and as the famous 'wet-liner' Vanguard/TR engine began to show its age) that the idea of a six-cylinder engine was accepted. Even then it was not economically feasible to design an entirely new engine, so in the time-honoured 'mechanical Meccano' method refined by so many British firms in the 1930s, it was decided to produce a six-cylinder version of the new overhead valve SC four-cylinder engine already in use in the Standard Eight and Ten. By making suitable alterations to the machine tooling, it proved to be possible to retain the same front end (timing cover) and rear end (flywheel face) designs, but to build engines either with four cylinders and three crankshaft bearings, or six cylinders and four crankshaft bearings.

The SC engine had been 803 cc at first, and was soon enlarged to 948 cc, but at that point (in the mid-1950s) no further enlargement of the capacity was foreseen. Accordingly, when Harry Webster's engineers produced the very first six-cylinder

version of it, the prototype had a 1422 cc capacity. However, since the sales department's first priority was to have a more refined engine in the Series III Vanguard, to replace the reliable but rather agricultural 2088 cc four-cylinder engine, the designs were further modified.

Harry Webster discovered a way of allowing for a considerably larger cylinder bore in the design, by shuffling the position of the cylinder walls relative to the cylinder head's holding down studs, and this immediately allowed the SC capacity to be pushed up to 1147 cc (with more in reserve), while the capacity of the new 'six' was pushed right out to 1998 cc for use in the Vanguard Six, announced in the autumn of 1960. This was done while retaining the same stroke of 76 mm (a dimension not changed until the arrival of the 2.5PI in 1968), and by enlarging the cylinder bore to 74.7 mm.

In the meantime, and in spite of the fact that Standard-Triumph was rapidly sinking into financial trouble, the directors were pushing ahead with the enlargement of the range of Herald-based cars. In September 1960 (actually at the same meeting as the approval for building the first Spitfire 'mock up' was made), the Board asked engineering to produce a longer, wider, four-door version of the Herald saloon, fitted with one of the six cylinder engines—this, incidentally, was something of a panic meas-

---

ABOVE RIGHT: *The car which made the idea of a six-cylinder Spitfire so very much more straightforward was the 1.6-litre Vitesse, announced in 1962. That's another false number plate—3VC properly belonged to a TR4 works rally car*

RIGHT: *The original Vitesse six-cylinder engine installation included twin semi-downdraught Solex carburettors and an air-cleaner underneath the carburettors*

ure, aimed at producing a cheap and cheerful successor to the ageing Vanguard. By March 1961, however, that scheme had been abandoned, and in its place approval was given to a new (and more rigid) rationalized chassis frame layout, known as the *Star* design, one version of which was to be fitted with a six-cylinder engine. It was at this point, only 14 months before the production car was revealed, that the Vitesse project crystalized.

I remember this project very clearly, as it was the first on which I worked when I joined the Standard-Triumph experimental department in the spring of 1961. Only a single prototype—a coupé, in fact, which was a version never sold to the public—had been constructed, and this was equipped with *two* nine gallon fuel tanks and was possessed of a phenomenal fuel range.

The Vitesse, when finalized, had a 1596 cc engine (a capacity achieved by reducing the Vanguard Six's cylinder bore to 66.75 mm), produced 70 bhp (net) at 5000 rpm with the aid of two semi-downdraught 32PHI Solex carburettors—as es-

pecially developed for the Vanguard Six—and had a close ratio gearbox cluster, without synchromesh on first gear, inside the existing Herald gearbox. The chassis-mounted final drive was pure Herald, and had a 4.11 : 1 ratio, but with more robust inner universal joints and fixings. Overdrive was made optional (such a fitting was never offered on the four-cylinder Herald), and Girling front disc brakes were standardized, allied to 8 × 1.25 in. rear brake drums. Getting the engine under the distinctive bonnet was something of an effort, and the radiator had to be pushed forward into the extreme nose, immediately behind the grille mesh.

At the launch, incidentally, number plate freaks were thoroughly confused to see Vitesses carrying 3VC and 4VC, which had already been seen on the

---

The competitions department occasionally rallied the Vitesses, which were nimble, but just not fast enough. This was Mike Sutcliffe in the 1963 Monte Carlo Rally

'works' Triumph TR4 rally cars in the Tulip Rally of 1962! The explanation was that the Vitesse numbers were fakes—the cars were not driven on the open road, and the plates just happened to be available in the experimental department (as the TR4s used plastic stick-on numbers!).

The Vitesse, therefore, went on to the market in May 1962 while the Spitfire was launched in October 1962. Both types were exported to North America as soon as possible, where the Spitfire retained its original name, but where the Vitesse was sold as the Sports Six. At this point, incidentally, I ought to kill the old canard that the original Spitfire was badged as a Spitfire 4 because Standard-Triumph were already planning to build a Spitfire 6. This simply is not true, and the truth is more prosaic. While the launch of the two new cars in the United States was being discussed, it had been decided to use *Sports Six* to badge the Vitesse. It therefore made a great deal of sense to call the true sports car not merely *Spitfire*, but *Spitfire 4*; that way, it was reasoned, the American buying public would realize that one car had a four-cylinder engine, and the other had six cylinders—there was nothing more complex than that.

At this point, too, I should emphasise just how many new models were being developed in the relatively small Standard-Triumph engineering division in the 1962–4 period. At this time I was running the re-formed competitions programme from a self-contained department at the back of the building, and can vouch for the fact that engine and transmission preparation work often had to wait for some engineering panic to subside. Apart from the ever-changing Herald/Vitesse scene, and the finalisation of the Spitfire project, the *Barb* programme (which became the Triumph 2000 in 1963) was going ahead full blast, the development of the all-

The later models of 1.6-litre Vitesse had a nicely-equipped fascia style, complete with rev-counter and wooden panel

independent suspension TR4A chassis had started, and the complex layout of the front-wheel-drive *Ajax* (Triumph 1300 in 1965) was being developed. Not only that, but the Spitfire racing and rallying programme (a major development exercise in itself) was also in full swing, and there were even thoughts of building a four-wheel-drive commercial vehicle using *Ajax* (Triumph 1300) engine and transmission components.

RIGHT: *The original Spitfire GT of 1963, by Michelotti, and with the style used unchanged for the GT6 of 1966. It was from this car that the Le Mans and team rally car fastback tops were moulded. There were no opening quarter windows on this prototype*

BELOW RIGHT: *The Spitfire GT of 1963, converted by Michelotti from a normal open Spitfire. The only changes made to the nose for production were to fit a new grille, and to eliminate the bonnet bulge*

BELOW: *False start—this was the Triumph Fury of 1965/66, with all-independent suspension and a 2-litre six-cylinder engine, all in a pressed-steel unit-construction bodyshell. Only one was built—it was too large, and looked like being too costly*

It was no wonder, therefore, that the evolution of the Spitfire sports car took something of a back seat almost as soon as the model had safely been put on the market. First thoughts on the further enlargement of the range came in 1963, when Harry Webster and Giovanni Michelotti got together, and decided to build what they called a 'Spitfire GT'. Quite simply, this was an unmodified Spitfire chassis, running gear, and most of the existing bodyshell, but it also had a new fixed-head, fastback, hardtop incorporating a lift-up hatch. During 1963, therefore, one of the original Spitfire prototypes—that carrying chassis no. X691, and registered 4305VC, which I had used as a 'chase car' on the 1962 RAC Rally—was sent out to Michelotti's studio in Turin for the conversion to be done.

The transformed machine, now painted bright red, returned to Coventry later in 1963 and—externally at least—it was in very much the same shape which the GT6 would adopt three years later. It was a sleek, refined, and very nicely trimmed Spitfire which soon made many friends among Triumph management. Right away, it became one of the select handful of experimental cars regularly used by the directors for overnight transport. (One

of these cars, incidentally, a particularly fast Vitesse-based machine, was so well-liked by Harry Webster that he tended to monopolise it, and it was soon unofficially christened the 'Kenilworth Dragster'.

Standard-Triumph's board of directors first discussed the 'Spitfire GT' project formally in August 1963, when the prototype had not yet been finished, and in December 1963 they were discussing a public launch timed for the autumn of 1964, but by May 1964 their ideas had been changed, and a six-cylinder engine had been installed. So, what happened? And what went wrong?

Intrinsically, there was nothing wrong with the way the prototype Spitfire GT behaved. There were, however, three important problems. In engineering terms, the advantage of the sleek new Michelotti-styled fastback was that it conferred a higher top speed on the Spitfire, but two disadvan-

RIGHT: *The Spitfire GT fascia style of autumn 1963, with more instruments than would be fitted to the GT6 production car.*

BELOW RIGHT: *At the same time as the GT6 was being developed, the mechanically-identical Vitesse 2-litre was also produced*

BELOW: *The GT6 engine and gearbox, ready for installation, complete with twin horizontal Zenith-Stromberg carburettors and all-synchromesh gearbox*

tages were that it was a considerably heavier bodyshell, and that this meant reduced acceleration and heavier fuel consumption.

The sales force were not at all impressed—they did not see how they could successfully sell a heavier, thirstier, more sluggish Spitfire at a considerable price premium—nor, to be frank, did they see a ready-made market for such a well-equipped hatchback with such a small engine.

It was in this way, almost by the process of managerial osmosis, that the idea of building a six-cylinder engined fastback Spitfire took shape, and since the principle of slotting six-cylinder engines into Herald-type chassis frames was already well established, there was no major installation problem to discourage the planners.

By the spring of 1964 the Spitfire GT had been given a six-cylinder 1596 cc Vitesse engine with two Zenith-Stromberg carburettors, though it retained the small-section Spitfire tyres and a 4.11:1 final drive ratio. This original engine, incidentally, produced 89 bhp with twin exhausts, but the change (for cost-control and installation reasons) to a single exhaust pipe, along with one or two other refinements meant that only 77 bhp was available. At this stage the doors had no swivelling quarter panes and one result was that the windows tended to be sucked out at high speed.

The author actually took X691 for its first long journey in this guise—to Le Mans, and to Paris, in June 1964, when it was necessary to show off the

proposed fastback Le Mans Spitfire style to the organizers to get their approval of certain dimensions. In the meantime, the specification of the Vitesse was coming under scrutiny, and the first industry rumours of a fastback/hatchback MGB were also beginning to circulate. Both these pressures eventually affected the development of the new six-cylinder Spitfire GT.

RIGHT: *GT6 Mk 1, with the optional wire-spoke wheels, on the grass of the Canley factory's sports field. In the background is the evidence of a Standard-Triumph factory which was positively booming with business in 1966*

BELOW RIGHT: *Open wide please—which shows how easy it was to stow anything into the loading area of the GT6*

BELOW: *One of the very first GT6s, being speed tested at MIRA by Fred Nicklin, and complete with the proper radiator grille*

At this point, however, I crave time for a slight diversion into whimsy. Standard-Triumph, as I have already made clear, were addicted to using project codes for their new designs. The Spitfire had always been known as *Bomb*, whereas the Vitesse had always been known as *Atom*. It is, however, a matter of historical fact that the six-cylinder Spitfire GT never had a code name—it took on the GT6 title at an early stage—and my own personal suggestion of 1964, that it should be known as *Atom Bomb*, was brushed aside. . . .

Changes would have to be made to the Vitesse, for this car was not selling as well as it should. Although it was adequately fast when launched during 1962, with a 1596 cc engine (its maximum speed) was about 87 mph, and its 0–60 mph acceleration about 17.5 seconds), it was not very economical, for 25 mpg was an average achievement, and it was rather sparsely equipped. Furthermore, it was not as well-liked as the Sunbeam Rapier of the day, which was an obvious competitor, and it became quite overshadowed by the

Ford Cortina GT when that model was revealed in the spring of 1963.

Hand-in-hand with the development of the GT6, therefore, it was decided to make the Vitesse not only faster, but better equipped, and more robust. There would not be any embarrassing overlap with more expensive Triumphs, for the old and out-of-date Vanguard had been replaced by the successful 2000 at the end of 1963. It was decided that both the new or modified Triumphs should be announced together—their public announcement, in fact, eventually taking place in the first week of October 1966. In every way, thank goodness, they were better than they might have been.

Most importantly, the original Vitesse's 1596 cc engine size was abandoned, and it was decided to settle on the 1998 cc six-cylinder engine, almost exactly in the same tune as that specified for the Triumph 2000; apart, indeed, from the raised compression ratio (9.5 : 1 in the Vitesse 2-litre/GT6 cars compared with 9.0 : 1 in the 2000), and amendments to the manifolding to suit the upright engine installation and the confines of the GT6's engine bay, the two engines were virtually identical.

Twin Zenith-Stromberg carburettors (which were constant-vacuum instruments of SU type, actually designed by Standard-Triumph engineers at the end of the 1950s, and subsequently sold to Zenith) were fitted. In GT6/Vitesse trim, peak power was 95 bhp (net) at 5000 rpm, just five bhp more than the power developed in the 2000 saloon.

Getting the lengthy six-cylinder engine into the GT6 and Vitesse engine bays meant that the radiator had to be pushed up to the absolute nose of the chassis. In the GT6, this resulted in a rather complex cooling system, which incorporated a filler cap remote from the radiator block itself. A slim air cleaner housing linked the two carburettors, and hung over the engine bay splash guard on the offside. To impart that sense of 'class', the engine's rocker cover was chrome plated.

Behind the engine, and in unit with it, the GT6 had an 8.5 in. diameter diaphragm spring clutch (that of the Spitfire was 6.5 in.) and a new all-synchromesh, close-ratio gearbox, with optional

RIGHT: *A bonnetful of engine in the original GT6, showing how the carburettors and air cleaner just overhang the splash guard on the right side of the engine bay*

BELOW: *The sleek lines of the GT6 admirably demonstrated by this overhead picture*

Laycock overdrive operating on top and third gears. As already mentioned in the previous chapter, this all-synchromesh box had been 'blooded' in the works Spitfires as early as 1964. Although it was of the constant-load, rather than the baulk-ring type of synchromesh, it was a more robust box than the original close-ratio installation of the 1.6-litre Vitesse, and fully capable of dealing with the GT6's power and torque delivery.

For interest, here are the internal ratios, compared with those of the 1.6-litre Vitesse:

GT6/Vitesse 2-litre box	(o/d 0.80), 1.00, 1.25, 1.78, 2.65, reverse 3.10:1
1.6-litre Vitesse box (no synchromesh on first gear)	(o/d 0.80), 1.00, 1.25, 1.78, 2.93, reverse 2.93:1

—some components, it may be inferred from a study of the figures, were the same as used on the previous box.

Although the chassis-mounted final drive and differential unit looked similar to the existing Spitfire/Herald/Vitesse 1600 unit, it was a new and more solid design. For the GT6 without overdrive, the ratio was normally 3.27:1 (36 crown wheel teeth, 11 pinion teeth, while if overdrive was fitted the ratio became 3.89:1 (35 crown wheel teeth, nine pinion teeth). On the Vitesse 2-litre, the axle ratio was always 3.89:1, whether or not overdrive was specified.

On the GT6 the spare wheel was stowed away under a hardboard panel in the loading floor, and was extracted through the hatchback door

The basic layout of the Spitfire was unchanged for the GT6, though there were changes to spring rates, damper settings and the size of the front anti-roll bar, while the steering ratio was reduced to give low efforts, there now being 4.25 turns from lock to lock of the 15 in. diameter leather-trimmed steering wheel.

Like the Spitfire, the GT6 was available with 4.5 in. rim centre-lock wire wheels, but unlike the Spitfire, the standard bolt on wheels had 4.5 in. rims as well, and 155-13 in. Dunlop SP41 radial tyres were standard. To keep the performance in check, there were bigger front disc calipers and 8 in. rear brake drums—the total brake swept area being 260 sq. in. compared with 199 sq. in. for the Spitfire.

Apart from the need to incorporate a long and sleek bonnet bulge to clear the contours of the six-cylinder engine, and to add a row of cooling louvres on each side of this (to ease the under-bonnet temperature problem), the GT6's body style was exactly like that proposed by Michelotti, and it incorporated several obvious recognition points. The sweeping fastback, of course, was quite unmistakeable, and the fact that the upward-opening hatchback had been ante-dated by the MGB GT did not mean that Triumph were playing copycat, for Michelotti had thought it all up in 1963, two whole years before the MGB GT had been launched.

At the front of the car, compared with the Spitfire, there was a different horizontally-slatted radiator grille and a different arrangement of side lamps and indicators, while at the rear the GT6 was given a pair of reverse lamps, inboard of the indicators. Because of the fastback coupé style, of course, it had been necessary to design a new 9.75 (Imp.) gallon fuel tank, which lived in the nearside of the boot floor, flanked by the spare wheel, and its filler cap was located on the nearside of the tail panel, just below the line of the hatchback aperture.

The big fastback roof pressing, incidentally, was supplied to Forward Radiator in Birmingham by Pressed Steel Co. at Oxford, but Forward Radiator looked after assembly of the body, which took place alongside, and intermingled with, the Spitfire shells. The hatchback, incorporating the large rear window, was hinged at the front, and rose with the aid of torsion bar assistance.

The wind down door glasses were supplemented on the GT6 by swivelling front quarter windows (which were never fitted to the cheaper Spitfire models), while behind the doors there were rear quarter windows, front hinged, which could also be latched open to encourage through-flow ventilation.

Inside the car, there was a well-equipped fascia and instrument panel, with a walnut veneer, Triumph 1300-style instruments (the rev-counter and speedometer being ahead of the driver's vision, rather than in the centre of the car as on the Spitfire), and other tasteful details. Pedals and steering column controls were the same as those of the Spitfire, but there were parcel shelves at each side of the fascia, above the passengers' legs, along with a padded grab handle for the passenger.

The floor was completely carpetted, there were carpetted kick-strips on the doors, and the bucket seats were firmly and tastefully padded. No attempt had been made to provide useless + 2 accomodation (the padded 'shelf' in the MGB GT was more an irritant than an asset). Instead there was a wooden floor panel above the spare wheel and fuel tank

which extended forward almost to the back of the seats, and two small open boxes were formed between this panel and the floor itself where valuables could approximately be stored out of sight.

Overall, the GT6 was definitely intended to be a fast little Grand Touring car (that, after all, was what the 'GT' initials stand for), rather than a sports car with a fixed roof, and this was reflected not only in the high standard of fittings, but in the suspension behaviour. Triumph had spent some time getting the sight, the sound *and* the feel of the first GT6s to their satisfaction. A look back to the *Autocar* impressions I penned in 1966 reminds me that I described the engine as being 'completely

The 'electrical' side of the GT6 engine, with dynamo, coil and distributor all in evidence

smooth and well silenced; on the move there is little more than a well-bred purr from under the bonnet. . . .' However, I also sounded the first published note of caution about the new car's behaviour, for I thought that, 'On smooth roads, even the handling reminds one of a Jaguar E-type. The rack and pinion steering is low geared so quite a lot of wheel-twirling is needed to hustle the little car around twisting lanes. Damper settings are definitely softer than those of the Spitfire, no doubt to provide a "boulevard" ride favoured by the Americans.'

Standard-Triumph had obviously spent some time agonising about the price, and eventually pitched it at £800 (basic) in Britain, which jumped to £985 if purchase tax was added. The GT6's obvious competitor was the MGB GT, which was priced at £1016, though it is interesting to note that the GT6 was priced at exactly the same level as the existing TR4A, and that the Spitfire Mk 2 sold for £678.

It was a car, too, which was rarely delivered in absolutely 'basic' form. *Autocar*'s 1967 test car was equipped with the fresh air heater (£13.50), safety belts (£8) and overdrive (£58.38), though the wire wheels at £36.88 were not fitted. Even without any extras, the GT6 weighed 1904 lb. ready for the road, which compares with 1568 lb. for the current Mk 2 Spitfire of the day. The power outputs, therefore, had been increased by 42 per cent, while the weight had gone up by only 21 per cent; even allowing for the 25 per cent higher gearing of the GT6 (and

closer ratio gears) compared with the Spitfire, the GT6 promised to have rather more performance than any previous small Triumph.

So far, so good. Following its launch, the GT6 generally received good preview comments from motoring writers. Most of them were perhaps over generously disposed towards its handling, while all seemed to love the styling, the refined, smooth, six-cylinder engine philosophy, and the level of equipment. The general public, it seemed, were equally impressed.

The first production cars were assembled in the summer of 1966 (nine in July, 17 in August, and 120 in September) but by the beginning of 1967 the build rate had settled down to between 500 and 600 a month. What is quite fascinating is that this rate was sustained, through controversy and model change, for the next five to six years. Nothing, it seemed, could bump up demand much higher, and nothing seemed to stop the little coupé from selling. For the record, the peak production month was May 1967, when 755 cars were built, followed by 721 in January 1970 and 702 in November 1968.

How did this compare with the Spitfire itself? Much of the time, when GT6s were being built at 500–600 a month, Spitfire production was about 1200–1500 a month. Both, of course, were highly creditable figures, and both must have been very profitable to the Standard-Triumph sector of Leyland/British Leyland at the time.

The sales force, the engineers and the directors, therefore, could afford to brush off the comments made by the road testers—for the moment at least. The problem was that most of them made the same sort of comments—that the performance was very good, that they liked the look of the car, but that they were rather unhappy about the handling. *Car*, that most forthright of British monthly magazines, pointed out that they, 'managed to provoke (the car) into a couple of fair old tail slides until a loud knocking noise from behind the seats discouraged us from trying harder.' Richard Bensted-Smith of *Motor*, trying a car at Mallory Park race circuit 'spent most of the time on the 180 degree south curve hovering between power-on and power-off in search of a neutral and predictable line.' *Modern Motor* of Australia were even more forthright, for they started their test with these words, 'Be warned. The Triumph GT6 suffers from the sudden onset of the dreaded swing-axle over steer. You must keep the power on through a corner or the back end acts like it is trying to nestle under an armpit.'

Only John Bolster of *Autosport* (who usually

Opening rear quarter windows were standardised for the GT6. The Spitfire GT prototype had not had such fittings

managed to say something nice about every car he drove), and *Road & Track* of the USA were impressed by the handling. *R & T* even went so far as to say that, 'We approach any car with conventional swing axles with a little apprehension, but we found that the GT6 could not be faulted on its handling. . . . Breakaway is smooth and one gets the feeling that the car has a degree of oversteer that can be enjoyed and utilised by a moderately skilled driver while never crossing up an unskilled one.'

Ho hum. What next? According to the factory, if the GT6 was properly set up, with negative camber to the rear wheels of between three and four degrees when laden, everything should be predictable. They did admit, privately *and* in public, that the damper settings were softer than for the Spitfire, and had been influenced by what Standard-Triumph Inc. had requested from North America. Even so, John Lloyd is still adamant that, 'there was no ordinary public reaction to the handling of the car, though the technical press criticised it. The Americans

never really objected, not at all—it never became an issue in the States. Then, of course, there was the usual Standard-Triumph problem that once the car was in production, engineering never had a lot of spare labour to do modifications. . . .'

It was a pity, in a way, that this aspect of the car's behaviour attracted so much attention, because there was so much that was good—very good— about the overall specification. The gearbox, for instance, not only had synchromesh on all forward gears, but it also had delightfully close ratios. It was deliberate policy to make the gearing *very* high in non-overdrive form—the 3.27:1 final drive ratio used was much higher than anything else in the Spitfire/GT6 range of differential units—so much so that the little car could achieve 46 mph in bottom gear and no less than 69 mph in second gear at the

The definitive GT6 fascia style and switchgear layout

recommended speed limit of 6000 rpm. This made open-road motoring in traffic on give-and-take roads quite delightful, and added to the charm of this compact little GT machine.

Even before it had been on sale for a year, the GT6 had established itself as a success. It was the only 'small six' in the business (in feel and refinement it left the rather lumpy old-fashioned MGB GT way behind). *Road & Track*, an influential voice among North American sports car

fans, summed it all up in two sentences, 'Something quite new and distinctive. . . . It has no parallel, and it's worth the money.'

Which was quite good enough for Standard-Triumph at the time. In any case, they were already proposing to do something about the handling when they could find the time. There was never enough of that—in 1967 they were finalizing the TR5/TR250 models, which would finally consign Standard's old 'wet-liner' four-cylinder engine to the parts catalogue, and transform the image of the broad-shouldered TR, and they had also updated the Spitfire in no uncertain manner. 1967 will go down in history as a very important year for Standard-Triumph, not only for the new models which appeared, or were developed, but for the fact that their owners, Leyland, at last got into serious negotiation with BMC. The future, all of a sudden, not only looked exciting, but uncertain as well. Where, if a merger came to pass, would a modified Spitfire fit in?

OPPOSITE PAGE: Squashy and comfortable (though rather narrow) seats in the original GT6 of 1966

BELOW: In the GT6 there was stowage space, not lockable but at least out of sight from prying eyes, under the loading floor in the tail

Facts and figures: GT6 (retrospectively called GT6 Mk 1)

Built   July 1966 to September 1968
Number built   15,818
Chassis numbers   KC 1 to KC 13752

Engine   6-cyl, in-line, cast-iron cylinder block and cylinder head, with four crankshaft main bearings. Bore, stroke and capacity 74.7 × 76 mm., 1998 cc (2.94 × 2.99 in., 122 cu. in.). CR 9.5:1, 2 Zenith-Stromberg carburettors. 95 bhp (net) at 5000 rpm. Maximum torque 117 lb. ft at 3000 rpm.

Transmission   Final drive ratio 3.27:1. Overall gear ratios 3.27, 4.11, 5.82, 8.66, reverse 10.13:1. With optional overdrive, final drive ratio 3.89:1. Overall ratios (o/d 3.11), 3.89. 4.86, 6.92, 10.30, reverse 12.06:1. Synchromesh on all forward gears. Overdrive (optional) on top and third gears. 20.1 mph/1000 rpm in direct top gear with overdrive not fitted; 21.2 mph/1000 rpm in overdrive top gear.

Basic prices   UK   £800
                 USA $2895

Suspension and brakes   9.7 in. front disc brakes, 8 × 1.25 in. rear drums. 155-13 in. radial ply tyres on 4.5 in. rim bolt-on steel disc wheels, or centre-lock wire-spoke wheels.

Dimensions   Length, 12 ft 1 in., width 4 ft 9 in.; height 3 ft 11 in. Front track 4 ft 1 in.; rear track 4 ft 0 in. Unladen weight 1904 lb.

Chapter 6
Spitfires 3 and IV: 1967 to 1974

Following the introduction of the GT6 coupé, the launch of an improved Spitfire was not delayed for long. The Spitfire was still selling very well, so there was no need to change the model merely to keep potential customers interested, but it found itself in a very competitive market sector. BMC were committed to making frequent changes to the Sprite/Midget, and it did not seem as if either concern would let an established model carry on for too long.

In January 1967, therefore, only two years since the last big change had taken place, the last Spitfire 2 was built at Canley, and a significantly improved Spitfire 3 took its place. Following the 45,753 Spitfire Mk 1s, a further 37,409 Spitfire Mk 2s had followed. In every sales year, so far, the Spitfire had outsold the Sprite and Midget models (combined together), a situation which Donald Stokes and the Leyland combine wanted to see continue.

In the design and development factory at the western end of the Canley complex, there had been a lot of activity in recent years. In 1965 the front-wheel-drive 1300 saloon had been put into production, along with the all-independent suspension TR4A and the Spitfire Mk 2. In the meantime, work had been going ahead on a new medium-size sports car design (the *Fury*), of which only one prototype was ever built, and on a brand-new family of overhead camshaft engines—a four-cylinder version originally for Saab's use, and later for Triumph, and a vee-8 for eventual use in the Stag. There had also been time to prepare the GT6, and the closely-related 2-litre Vitesse.

Triumph's engineering facility was incredibly energetic at this time. Even though it was generally understood by the engineers, the sales force, and the directors, that the next version of the Spitfire would have a larger and more powerful derivative of its existing Herald-based engine, Harry Webster and John Lloyd still found time for a diversion.

Early in 1966—only a year, in fact, after the first test-bed engines began to run—a Mk 1 Spitfire was carved about so that a development example of the brand-new 'PE150' overhead cam slant-four engine could be fitted, and tested. It was all very tentative, and premature (the supply of engines, not even meant to go into production until 1968, was all promised to Saab at first, for their new Type 99 saloon), but it seemed like a good idea at the time.

'We built this one slant-4 Saab-engined Spitfire, with a 1700 cc engine size. It wasn't an easy engine to get in, because it was designed to lie over at 45 degrees. We got it in—just—but it was an expensive carve-up. There were chassis frame changes, bonnet changes, scuttle changes, but what really swayed a decision against it was not that the customers didn't want more performance in the States, but because the car was not competitive enough—it would have cost too much money.

'Incidentally, it went like a bomb—a *Bomb*, yes!— it was a nice motor car, and it would have been OK for exhaust emissions, but we never persevered.'

A performance test of that car (registered 248KV) was carried out in May 1966, where, at MIRA, it recorded 98 mph with the standard 4.11:1 final drive ratio, and completed the quarter mile in 18.65 seconds.

In place of this interesting car, the pragmatic, if less sensational, decision was merely to improve the existing Spitfire, and to make it more suitable for the ever-burgeoning safety laws being introduced in the United States. (In case anyone still believes that too much notice was being taken of North American

Apart from the raised bumper position, the Mk 3 was also distinguished by the use of a folding hood which stowed away in a pouch when furled

conditions, I should point out that in 1965 and 1966 the proportion of 'export' sales to total sales of Spitfires was 78.3 and 74.1 per cent respectively—and that the vast majority of these sales were made in North America. If the Spitfire had only concentrated on the British market it would not have been a viable proposition, as annual sales in the mid-1960s averaged about 4500 cars a year.) Cost, the shortage of time, and tooling considerations meant that the basic chassis, mechanical, suspension and body layouts could not be changed, but that every detail of the design could receive attention.

The original Herald engine had been enlarged to 1147 cc for 1961, but soon after this further enlargement was considered. Even when the fwd Triumph 1300 was still just a sketch on the drawing boards—in 1962—the use of an overbored 1296 cc version had been settled for the model. It was not, however, as simple as that, for the 1300 was also given an eight-port cylinder head (948 cc and 1147 cc quantity-production engines had six-port heads, with siamezed inlet ports), in which the joint to the revised cylinder block was ensured by ten holding down studs instead of 11 studs.

The eight-port quantity-production head, therefore, was obviously and completely different from the competition heads used on the 1964–5 race and rally Spitfires, though all the experience gained in that application was fed into the final version of it. In the case of the front-drive 1300, the new engine had a bore of 73.7 mm instead of 69.3 mm, and an unchanged stroke of 76 mm, used a cast-iron single outlet exhaust manifold, and a cast-alloy inlet manifold, without water-heating, and with a single 1.5 in. Zenith-Stromberg carburettor. For the Spitfire Mk 3, however, something much more ambitious could be provided. The same Mk 2 camshaft profile was retained, but the tubular exhaust manifold of the Mk 2 was abandoned in favour of a new cast iron component, and there was a new water-heated alloy inlet manifold fed by two horizontal 1.25 in. SU carburettors.

Power curves released by Standard-Triumph at the time of the launch revealed not only that peak power, compared with the Mk 2, had been increased from 67 bhp (net) at 6000 rpm, to 75 bhp (net) at the same figure, but that the torque was up from 67 lb. ft at 3750 rpm to 75 lb. ft at 4000 rpm.

Even that was not the end of the story, for the larger, 1296 cc, engine was clearly lustier at all engine speeds. At only 1000 rpm, for instance—a very low engine speed for a sports car—the torque had been increased from 13 lb. ft to 25 lb. ft, which demonstrated how much more flexible the new car would be to drive.

Apart from the use of a more robust 6.5 in. diameter diaphragm spring clutch to deal with this increased engine performance, no other drive line changes were made at this time. The final drive ratio remained at 4.11 : 1, and overdrive (operating on top and third gears) was still optional.

The chassis and running gear was only improved in detail. No improvement was made to the steel disc wheels, which still had ridiculously narrow 3.5 in. rims, and cross-ply tyres were still standard, though 4.5 in. centre-lock wire wheels were optional, (for £36.87), as were 145-13 in. Dunlop SP41 radial ply tyres for both types of wheel. Front disc calipers were enlarged to the latest Girling 14LF Mk 3 type, very similar to those already specified for the Triumph 1300 saloon. They featured slightly larger pads with a bigger volume—this being one of the minor, but direct, benefits of a serious competition programme. The steering, with well over four turns

lock-to-lock to achieve that remarkable 24 ft turning circle, was not changed either, but the Mk 3 had a new 15 in. steering wheel with sprung spokes, which was actually the same as that currently in use for the TR4A.

A minor point, but one which is often ignored by restorers of Spitfires, is that the Mk 3 was the first derivative to have negative earth electrical fittings, and that this made almost every electrical item on the car different from those used on the Mk 2.

The more noticeable changes were those made to the body work. The major difference was at the front of the car, where a new bumper blade was mounted squarely ahead of the front grille (rather than below it, as on earlier cars), and given rubber-tipped under-riders. This almost immediately became known as the 'bone-in-the-teeth' style, which was only to be modified in detail in the next 13 years. There were new combined side lamp/indicator units positioned below the bumper, at each side of the grille, and re-shaped rear quarter bumpers to suit the section of the new blades.

Other new details included the use of twin circular reverse lamps on the tail, immediately inboard of the indicators, and a wooden fascia panel surrounding an unchanged instrument layout.

Functionally, however, the big improvement was to weather protection. Out went the original 'build-it-yourself, slot-it-in' hood and sticks, and in its place, came a proper fold-away hood. When furled, it lived neatly in a pouch around the rim of the passenger compartment, and when erect it clipped snugly to the screen rail with a pair of over-centre catches.

The new raised front bumper position had not been chosen merely to make the car look different (although it most certainly did so), but to help the car comply with new American proposed bumper-height regulations. It must have been to the Spitfire Mk 3's credit that it also took on a touch of the looks of the Lotus Elan, even if its performance did not quite match that of the Elan.

Performance. Ah, yes, performance. According to predictions, the Mk 2 Spitfire should have been capable of 96 mph, and on the same basis this Mk 3 car should have been able to reach 100 mph. A 100 mph Spitfire would have been good to advertise—but unfortunately not all the press cars could do the job for the factory. *Motor*'s test car, complete with wind-smoothing hardtop option (£28 extra on the basic price, now set at £582) could only reach 95 mph in direct top (overdrive gearing allowed 94 mph to be achieved), while

---

OPPOSITE PAGE: *Few changes for the Mk 3 Spitfire, except for the use of a wooden-veneer instrument panel and the sprung-spoke (TR4-type) steering wheel. The radio fitting was extra*

BELOW: *Wire-spoke wheels, with knock-on ears, continued to be options on Mk 3 Spitfires*

Autocar's car, tried in 1969, was only good for 92. Over in the United States, however, *Road & Track* carried out a double test (along with the latest Midget) in September 1967, and announced a top speed of 100 mph.

That, however, did not detract from the car's appeal. Even though the new version of the car was faced with stiffer Sprite/Midget competition than ever before (there was no doubt that the fitment of the de-tuned Mini-Cooper S 1275 cc engine for the Mk III Midget/Mk IV Sprite, for 1967, had attracted new custom), it still continued to out-sell the Abingdon product. In 1967 the advantage to the Spitfire was only 486 cars, but in 1968 it rose dramatically to no fewer than 5178 cars.

It was, however, a slightly confusing time for Triumph sports car customers, for the Spitfire was not, at this time, allowed to improve at the same time as the GT6 did so. When the GT6 became a Mk 2, in the autumn of 1968, a changed distinguished by the fitting of a more advanced lower-wishbone rear suspension, no change was made to the Spitfire. Magazine testers began to make more and more barbed references to the handling of the Spitfire, and to publish embarrassing pictures showing just how far the rear wheels could be made to tuck-under when the car was being cornered hard. *Autocar*, in a double test with the latest Midget, stated (in April 1969) that, 'Although we have no wish to malign the reputation of this very pleasant sports car, we make no apology for referring to its handling limitations. Its stablemates, the GT6 and Vitesse, now have a completely redesigned rear suspension system. What a pity that the Spitfire has not been included.'

To add to the slight air of confusion among Spitfire enthusiasts, there was also the fact that for North America, an entirely new fascia layout had been adopted for 1969 model-year cars (the left-hand-drive version of that to be standardized on all Mk IV models) but it was never applied to the British and European Mk 3s.

It was nearly time, indeed, for a major change to be brought into production, but first there was time for cosmetic improvements. For the 1970 model year, and coinciding with changes also being made to the GT6, the Mk 3 Spitfire received a new and more sporty steering wheel, improved cockpit padding, a matt black windscreen surround, new badging, and a detachable rear window panel in the folding hood. Of more importance, however, was that the standard steel wheels now had 4.5 in. instead of 3.5 in. rim widths—a long overdue

change—though there was no change to the standard tyre section. At the same time, and not only because the specification had been improved, the basic price of the car rose from £597 to £633—an increase of £36. This compared with £530 when the original Spitfire was launched in 1962; it was a £103, or 19 per cent increase in seven years. If only such days of ultra-low inflation could return!

(Similar cosmetic changes, incidentally, were made to the Sprite/Midget models at the same time, which resulted in both these cars finally being priced at the same level of £625. The difference in price was so small by this time that its effect on sales could virtually be ignored.)

The effort, clearly, was worth making. In 1969 the Sprite/Midget models outsold the Spitfire for the only time in their history—by just 640 cars—but in 1970 Triumph re-dressed the balance, and outsold Abingdon by 938 cars. 1970, too, was the year in which the Austin-Healey name was finally dropped—the Sprites built in 1971 were all badged as plain Austins, and from then on the Spitfire met the MG Midget on its own, in a straight fight.

In the meantime, momentous commercial events had taken place. After Triumph's owners, Leyland, had completed the takeover of Rover-Alvis in the spring of 1967, Sir Donald Stokes and his colleagues looked around for further firms to absorb. As the whole world surely now knows, they eventually bit off much more than they could chew for, helped along by a sympathetic British government, they

eventually merged with the BMH conglomerate (which effectively meant BMC-Jaguar), and in the spring of 1968 the new British Leyland Motor Corporation came into existence. At a stroke, therefore, it meant that Triumph were no longer in direct and bitter competition for sales with MG at Abingdon. Theoretically, at least—for in the next two or three years there was no sign, publicly or behind closed doors, that any attempt was being made to help Triumph and MG to work together.

Immediately this affected Triumph's personalities. Sir Donald Stokes relinquished direct control of the fortunes of Standard-Triumph, and moved Harry Webster and George Turnbull over to Longbridge to try to knock the ailing Austin-Morris combine into shape. Sir Donald remained as titular head of Standard-Triumph, with George Turnbull as his deputy, Lyndon Mills soon became sales director, while Spen. King, that exceptional engineer who had designed all the gas-turbine cars at Rover, and the still-to-be-seen Range Rover, took over from Harry Webster in engineering; John Lloyd moved up, and became his official deputy.

Even before the merger took effect, Triumph had been looking at ways of making really significant changes to the Spitfire/GT6 models for the 1970s. Dealers were making it very clear that although the cars were still selling very well, some customers were on their third or fourth Spitfires, and were beginning to look askance at buying yet another of the same style of cars.

In 1968, therefore, the Torinese stylist, Giovanni Michelotti, was asked to look again at the bodyshell, to leave the basic layout, all the centre panels, and most of the inner panels alone, but to propose what would be the first major re-style to this little two-seater. He had already had a frenetic few years on Triumph's behalf, for his own superb Stag concept had been followed by the changes being planned for the 1300 (they became the Toledo and 1500 models of 1970), and by the deft re-shaping of the Triumph 2000 saloon. He had been so busy, in fact, that the transformation of the TR5/TR250 into the TR6 had had to be contracted out, to Karmann of West Germany. Indeed, it was Karmann's clever re-style of the TR5 shape—they transformed the front and the tail of the car without altering the main cockpit area—which inspired Triumph's directors to ask the same of Michelotti for the Spitfire.

Triumph archive pictures, one of which I have been allowed to use in this book, showed that

---

BELOW LEFT: *Compared with the earlier types, almost no changes to the boot space of the Mk 3 Spitfire, though the hood sticks no longer had to be stowed away around the fuel tank*

BELOW: *The Spitfire's handling problem, when cornered really hard, is evident here, for in this Silverstone demonstration drive the left side rear wheel is beginning to tuck under, and the right side wheel is almost at the limit of its travel.*

Michelotti proposed a new chopped-off tail which would carry the same styling theme as the Stag, the Triumph 2000, and the TR6 models, and linked it with a new droop-snoot bonnet style which incorporated fold-away headlamps mounted a few inches inboard of the modified wing-top crown line. The headlamps were carried, face-down behind flush covers, in the day time, but at night would have somersaulted upwards, like those on the Lotus Elan model—and they might also have been able to be flipped up rapidly, for flashing warnings during the day. It was a very neat scheme, which

incorporated a new and shallow full width grille, allied to wrap-around lamp fittings at the front corner of the car, and a new bumper profile to suit.

Everyone liked it—there was never any question about that—and it was formally put to the directors for approval in December 1968. Soon after that, however, the nose re-style was effectively abandoned, and never re-appeared during the life of the Spitfire. The reason, very simply, was that Triumph were frightened that proposed new legislation in the United States would outlaw hidden headlamps. The new laws had not then been enacted, but were threatened. The time lag between committing a new set of pressings to production, and actually getting them on sale, was such that Triumph might *just* have been ready to start selling droop-snoot Spitfires and GT6s when their use in North America became illegal. Europe's motor industry, at this time, was very wary of anything which might become law in North America and tried to steer well clear of such problems. We all know, now, that such

RIGHT: *Customised Spitfire—1968 variety*

BELOW: *For 1969, Triumph sold the Spitfire in North America with special badging, and with these unique wheel trims. Keith Hopkins (in dark suit) and Graham Whitehead (of ST's North American subsidiary) are behind the car*

headlamps were never outlawed, but at the time the risk could not be taken.

Michelotti was therefore told, most regretfully, that his neat sloping style could not be used. The ideas it contined might, one day, be used elsewhere. (They were, on his first attempts to style the TR7.) In place of this he was invited to produce a more conventional style with exposed headlamps, but one which would nevertheless blend with the chopped off tail, and the raised windscreen, of the rest of the re-shaping job.

The new nose finally adopted, which was also shared with the GT6 Mk 3, looked superficially

The simple swing axle independent rear suspension of the Spitfire was dropped when the Mk IV was announced in 1970; this was the ingenious, but effective, swing-spring derivative which replaced it

similar to the existing shape, but although it retained the same chassis pivots under the nose, and picked up at the same patented over-centre fixing handles ahead of the doors, it was entirely different in detail. The wing-top exposed panel seams had disappeared, and inward-turning seams were now along the side of the front wings, for the GT6 there was a re-profiled bonnet bulge to clear the longer six-cylinder engine, and the headlamp treatment was different. In addition there was a new slim-line bumper, new lower panel, and a distinctive grille. Big plastic bumpers set off the new look.

For the Spitfire only (the GT6, of course, kept its fastback hardtop, though in a revised style), there was a new and flatter boot lid, sweeping back to the edge of the chopped-off tail, with nicely integrated tail lamp/indicator/stop lamp/reverse lamp clusters. The rear of the car, indeed, looked much smarter than before. Integrating nicely with these changes were new-style road wheels, with neat centres and

exposed chrome-plated wheel nuts; centre-lock wire wheels were optional, as usual. The later USA-market Mk 3s had had rather unsatisfactory radial-style wheels, so these neat new designs, which were visually like those fitted to the current TR6 model, were a great improvement. The other minor change, made necessary by legislation, but an improvement for all that, was that recessed trigger-type door handles had taken the place of the twist-type handles fitted to all previous Spitfires.

To match the new body lines, Triumph also offered a new style of optional hardtop. In place of the bulbous little top which had been offered for all Spitfires built between 1963 and 1970, there was a new and more angular style, with more glass area. This, by the way, had been styled entirely in Coventry, and did not even originate, in sketch form, from the Michelotti studio.

This re-style, and the additional changes described below, were designed specifically to be phased in at the start of 1971 model-year sales in North America, which meant that the Canley assembly lines had to start building the cars before the end of 1970. For that reason, and because the last series of Mk 3 cars would be built after production of the new car, called Mk IV, had begun, Triumph were not anxious that the new cars should be seen at the Earls Court Motor Show in October 1970. They therefore chose the very oddest moment—the second week of the Earls Court Show, to announce the new cars. Like many things done by the publicity staff of British Leyland at this time, it was a muddled decision, misunderstood by almost everyone; instead of making its world debut in London, which would have been right, the Mk IV

The 100,000th Spitfire was built in February 1968, and was driven off the production by George Turnbull

Spitfire was seen in public, for the first time, in Turin two weeks later. For Michelotti himself, that was nice, but for the British customers, it was just pathetic.

The Mk 3 Spitfire, therefore, was superseded for 1971, after 65,320 examples had been built. This made it the most popular Spitfire so far, by quite a wide margin—the 100,000th Spitfire, in fact, had been driven off the production lines by George Turnbull with a real flourish on 8 February 1968, at which junction no fewer than 45,000 cars had gone to the United States and 25,000 to Europe. The Mk IV, though clearly still the same basic sports car, was better in many ways.

Mechanically, the good news was that there had been a dramatic improvement in the engineering of

the rear suspension, and an all-synchromesh gearbox had been standardized. At last, after so many years of criticism from the technical press, Triumph had altered their rear suspension, and produced a much better system without spending a fortune on it.

Perhaps some of the press had expected the Mk IV Spitfire to pick up the lower-wishbone suspension from the GT6 Mk 2, and it is true that for a time Triumph had been tempted to do just that, but cost considerations finally ruled it out. Instead, the swing-spring system invented so many years earlier, but never applied to a production car, was tried again, refined, and fitted to the Mk IV Spitfire.

The appeal of a swing-spring layout was its simplicity. The basic geometry of the system was not changed, and single-pivot swing axles were retained. With a swing-spring layout, however, the entire transverse half-elliptic leaf spring was allowed to pivot about its central mounting above the

---

The underside of the Spitfire was smooth, and protected all mechanical components except the sump pan itself from serious rough-road damage

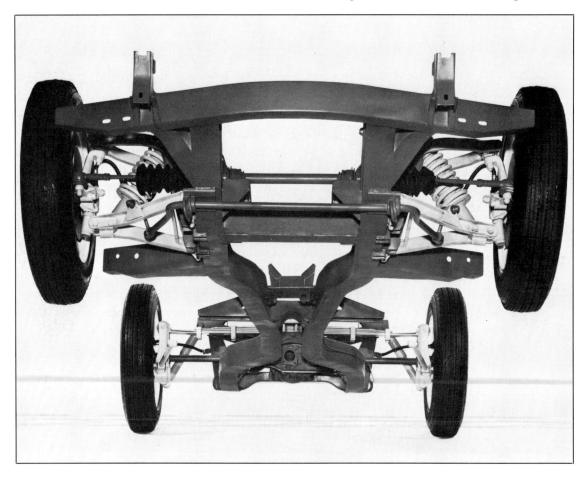

final drive. This meant that when the entire body/chassis unit began to roll—in other words, when going round a corner—the roll-stiffness was very small, as the spring pivotted in the opposite direction (in effect, that is, for in fact it stayed sensibly parallel to the road surface). It meant that the stiffness in 'single-bump' conditions was still adequate, but that in roll the tendency of the rear wheels to adopt strange camber angles, and to tuck under, was dramatically reduced. To achieve a satisfactory handling balance, however, the front suspension was fitted with a much stouter anti-roll torsion bar.

There was no major change to the 1296 cc engine for Europe, except that the power output was eventually recalibrated to a mere 63 bhp (DIN) at 6000 rpm. In the United States, however, as recounted in Chapter 8, the 1296 cc was already suffering slow but progressive strangulation from ever-tightening exhaust emission regulations. In 1969 and 1970 the Mk 3's peak output had dropped

to 68 bhp (with only a single Zenith-Stromberg carburettor in 1970), while for the first year of Mk IV production that was cut yet again to 58 bhp at 5200 rpm, still with a single emission-controlled Zenith-Stromberg carburettor. Worse was to come.

When the rear-drive Toledo had been announced in August 1970, with an all-synchromesh gearbox based on the casing of the Vitesse/GT6 design, it was clear that such a change to the Spitfire would soon follow. The same basic gearbox was adopted for the new Mk IV, and this gave the Spitfire an obvious and clear advantage over the Midget, which had to soldier on with a 'crash' first gear for another four years. Harry Webster once told me that the change from non-synchronized to synchronized first gear

---

The 75 bhp (net) Mk 3 engine was fitted with yet another version of the twin-SU carburettor installation, for an eight-port cylinder head had been adopted, and there were new inlet and (cast) exhaust manifolds

was made quite simply, by adding $\frac{5}{8}$th of an inch to the length of the main casing, and by retaining all other major gears, bearings, and synchromesh cones. First gear ratio was higher than before—3.50:1 instead of 3.75:1 inside the box. At the same time the final drive ratio was also raised from 4.11:1 to 3.89:1—this was a ratio which the rally team had

LEFT: *As early as 1965, this flip-up headlamp style was proposed for a Spitfire face lift, though at this time the exposed-seam bonnet was still to be retained. A modified version was proposed again in 1968, but dropped because of fears about future USA safety legislation*

BELOW: *Late model Mk 3 Spitfires had this type of fascia style, but only in left-hand-drive form for North America. It was finally adopted for all Spitfires intended for every market, with the introduction of the Mk IV model in 1970*

been using as long ago as 1964.

Inside the passenger compartment, the Mk IV was given a simplified, but very smart, version of the GT6 style, which is to say that the speedometer and rev-counter dials found themselves behind the steering wheel, ahead of the driver's eyes, whereas on all previous Spitfires they had been mounted in the central binnacle. On the Mk IV, therefore, they swooped sides along with the steering wheel. There was also a heater quadrant with proper slide controls (but it was still a water-valve heater), and the steering wheel had satin-finish spokes.

All in all, the Mk IV was a much better car than the Mk 3 which it replaced, though Triumph were very reluctant to admit that to meet various regulations they had had to trade off some of the performance of the superseded Mk 3. It went on sale in Britain before the end of 1970, priced at £735 (basic), compared with £669 for the last of the Mk 3s. Perhaps Triumph would not have made

such a big price increase (the extra £66 was an extra 10 per cent in one jump) if they had had their own way. Since 1968, British Leyland corporate policy had firmly been in command. The technically-inferior MG Midget, already priced at £692, had to be considered, and given a chance to survive.

Because Triumph were not too dependent on British and European sales of Spitfires to keep the production lines busy, they were presumably not too perturbed by the loss of performance between Mk 3 and Mk IV models, most of which had been caused by the commonisation of some components with the North American specification cars, and by the

---

Michelotti's hidden-headlamp suggestion could not be adopted, so a completely revised bonnet, smoother and with relocated seams, was designed for the Mk IV, and was accompanied by large plastics under-riders

higher gearing. The fact of the matter, however, is that *Autocar* could only achieve 90 mph in their Mk IV, while *Motor*, testing the same car five months later, only notched up 91 mph. All acceleration times, too, were worse than before, though day-to-day fuel consumption was as good as ever.

None of this, however, was thought too damaging, for every authoritative magazine test concentrated on the improvement in the handling brought about by the swing-spring rear suspension. *Autocar* said that this 'transforms the Spitfire's handling. . . . One of the most impressive things about the latest Spitfire is to be able to hurl it into a corner, lift off—and find the car still pointing where the driver aimed it. It seems almost impossible now to get the back wheels to tuck under and flick the car into a potentially frightening oversteer situation.' *Motor* thought the Mk IV's cornering behaviour 'safe and predictable'. After trying the Mk IV at Silverstone, *Motor Sport*'s Jeremy Walton reported that the handling was 'beyond reproach'; better yet, their august editor, Bill Boddy, thought that although: 'I note that J W says Spridgets can still run rings round the Spitfire, for road use I regard the Triumph as more of a motor car, as it has larger

dimensions. . . .' The Americans were no less enthusiastic, for *Road Test* thought the suspension much improved, as did the other publications.

The problem for Triumph was that other defects were beginning to be noticed, and brought forward for criticism, notably the hard ride, the low geared (Herald-ratio) steering, and the rattles and creaks which seemed to be endemic with this type of chassis and body construction. Neither did it help, for a time, that the specification actually seemed to degrade gradually for a time in the early 1970s.

In 1972 the latest exhaust emission regulations

LEFT: *The most prominent features of the re-skinned Spitfire Mk IV were the chopped-off tail, with a much flatter boot lid, and (optionally) the more angular hardtop, along with the full-width rear bumper*

BELOW LEFT: *Among the recognition points of the Spitfire Mk IV were the new exposed-nut road wheels, and the recessed door handles*

BELOW: *The new angular hardtop looked good from any angle*

cut such a swathe through the tune of the North American-specification Spitfire engine, that the peak power output was a mere 48 bhp (net) at 5500 rpm, and to give the car any sort of respectable performance the final drive ratio had to be dropped back to its original 4.11 : 1 figure. In the same year the fact that radial ply tyres became standard on British-market cars was merely balanced by the fact that the fuel tank was reduced in capacity to 7.25 gallons (but 8.75 gallons for the North Americans).

For North America the performance problem was so serious that the engine had to be enlarged once more—to 1493 cc—and this ensured that the specification of 'Federal' and British-market cars would differ widely in 1973 and 1974. The evolution of this power unit, however, is covered fully in

Chapter 9. In Britain, and for the rest of the world, the 1296 cc engine size was retained until the end of Mk IV production, towards the end of 1974.

In 1973 Triumph made a determined attempt to improve the appeal of their sports car range, by making changes to all three models—Spitfire, GT6 and TR6—at the same time. The Spitfire received a modified rear suspension, still of swing-spring type, but now with a track increase of two inches (and at the same time the GT6 lost its special lower-wishbone suspension, and took the new wide-track

This time the Spitfire isn't posed with a Spitfire aircraft—that is a 1930s Tiger Moth, with the new Mk IV

swing-spring suspension in its place), fire-retardant upholstery, reclining seats, a smaller steering wheel, re-styled instruments and a wooden-faced instrument panel instead of the original matt-black panel.

Later in 1973 the centre-lock wire wheel option was abandoned, and in August the original D-type overdrive was displaced by the new-model LH-type overdrive. For 1974 an under-bumper spoiler was added to the specification, and in the middle of that year the tonneau cover, previously optional on all Spitfires, was standardized.

By this time, however, the British seemed to be losing interest in the Spitfire. The smart revision in the looks, from Mk 3 to Mk IV, had only worked for a couple of years, after which the decline set in with a vengeance. Home sales were 5328 in 1971, and 7077 in 1972 (that was the year in which the Americans gave the thumbs-down to the 48 bhp 1296 cc Spitfire, which meant that more production capacity could be released for home-market cars), but they fell to 4082 in 1973, and to a mere 2743 in 1974.

Was the Spitfire finally dying off, and was the decline terminal? Only a determined effort to market the faster, and better, 1975 1500 model would reverse the trend.

The engine of the Mk IV of November 1970, very similar to the Mk 3, with the large alternator prominent, and the carburettor air hoses at the other side. Radial ply tyres were standard

Facts and figures: Spitfire Mk 3

Built   January 1967 to December 1970

Number built   65,320

Chassis numbers   FD1 to FD15306, FD20000 to FD51967. Then, from October 1969, FD75000 to FD92803 inclusive.

Engine   4-cyl, in-line, cast-iron cylinder block and (eight-port) cylinder head, three crankshaft main bearings. Bore, stroke and capacity 73.7 × 76 mm., 1296 cc (2.90 × 2.99 in., 79.1 cu. in.). CR 9.0:1, 2 SU carburettors. 75 bhp at 6000 rpm. Maximum torque 75 lb. ft at 4000 rpm.

Transmission   Final drive ratio 4.11:1. Overall gear ratios 4.11 (3.37 in optional overdrive top), 5.74, 8.88, 15.42, reverse 15.42:1. Synchromesh on top, third and second gears; optional overdrive, operating on top and third gears. 15.7 mph/1000 rpm in direct top gear; 19.1 mph/1000 rpm in overdrive top.

Basic prices   UK   £582 at first, £597 from July 1968, £633 from October 1969, £649 from February 1970, £669 from July 1970

USA $2199 (1967), $2235 (1968), $2295 (1969), $2395 (1970).

Suspension and brakes   9.0 in. front disc brakes, 7 × 1.25 in. rear drums. 520-13 in. tyres on 3.5 in. rim bolt-on steel disc wheels or 4.5 in. rim centre-lock wire-spoke wheels; 4.5 in. rim steel disc wheels from start of 1970 model year.

Dimensions   Length 12 ft 1 in.; width 4 ft 9 in.; height 3 ft 11.5 in. Front track 4 ft 1 in.; rear track 4 ft 0 in. Unladen weight (basic specification) 1568 lb.

Facts and figures: Spitfire Mk IV

Built   November 1970 to December 1974

Number built   70,021

Chassis numbers   FH3 to FH64,995 (Home Market) (FK prefix for USA, FL prefix for Sweden, FM prefix for USA 1500s, 1973–4)

General   The Mk IV had a completely re-skinned body style, with seamless bonnet, cut-off 'corporate-style' tail, and optional angular-style hardtop. Swing-spring rear suspension was adopted, along with all-synchromesh gearbox.

Technical specification as for Spitfire Mk 3 except for:

Engine   63 bhp (DIN) at 6000 rpm. Maximum torque 69 lb. ft at 3500 rpm.

Transmission   Final drive ratio 3.89:1. Overall gear ratios 3.89 (3.12 in optional overdrive top), 5.41, 8.41, 13.65, reverse 15.0:1. Synchromesh on all forward gears; optional overdrive operating on top and third gears. 16.7 mph/1000 rpm in direct top gear; 20.8 mph/1000 rpm in overdrive top gear.

Basic prices   UK   £735 at first, rising steadily to £1163 by Autumn 1974

USA $2649 (1971), $2699 (1972), $2995 (1973), $3345 (1974).

Suspension and brakes   Rear suspension basically as for Mk 3, but with pivotting-spring leaf spring location. 9.0 in. front disc brakes, 7 × 1.25 in. rear drums. 145-13 in. radial ply tyres on 4.5 in. rim bolt-on steel wheels or centre-lock wire-spoke wheels.

Dimensions   Length 12 ft 5 in.; width 4 ft 10.5 in.; height 3 ft 11.5 in. Front track 4 ft 1 in.; rear track 4 ft 0 in. (4 ft 2 in. from Chassis No. 50001, February 1973). Unladen weight (basic specification) 1717 lb.

ABOVE LEFT: *Mk IV at speed at Silverstone, with Ray Henderson in the passenger seat, and a satisfied press man enjoying the transformed handling capabilities*

LEFT: *The 1973-model face lift for Spitfire Mk IVs included this under-bonnet front spoiler*

Chapter 7
Mark 2 and Mark 3: the GT6 benefits

Just two years after the original GT6 was first shown, the Mk 2 GT6 was revealed. With no more than a handful of minor, significant, but deft engineering changes, Triumph now offered a much-improved machine. It was a real transformation. In truth, I have never known any other new version of an existing car which silenced its original critics so completely. It was almost as if the decision makers in Coventry had collected every GT6 road test ever published—domestic, or from export markets—had sifted through all the comments, and set out to deal with every one of the criticisms. The differences in behaviour between the GT6 Mk 1 and the GT6 Mk 2 were very obvious; the problem was that it made virtually no difference to sales!

It was a faster car than before, with better ventilation, and improved equipment. The major advance, however—and one made with very little alteration to the established design—was in the rear suspension area. As ever, it was Harry Webster, the technical director who couldn't keep away from drawing boards, who had sketched up the original idea, though his chassis designers take much of the credit for keeping the costs and complications to such a low level.

As Harry Webster recently told me, 'The GT6's performance, and indeed that of the Vitesse and Spitfire, had out-paced the original Herald type of rear suspension which was, don't forget, *the* cheapest form of independent rear suspension we could devise at the time. First of all, to improve matters, we invented the swing-spring system which eventually found its way on to the Spitfire (that was an idea of Mick Bunker's, by the way), then we went on to an even better system, the lower-wishbone layout. It had to be very simply done, for what you have to remember is that the company was never over-generous with tooling money, so large modifications were considered impractical. I suppose you could say that it *was* my bright idea in the first place, but that sort of change used to evolve by a process of discussion, and full-size sketching.'

In fact, the ingenious new suspension layout finally chosen for the GT6 coupé was initially conceived for the Vitesse saloon, where the swing-axle oversteer problem was more acute. Later, indeed, the new layout was proposed for fitment to the Vitesse, the GT6 and the Spitfire. Certainly, by the autumn of 1967, only a year after the original GT6 and Vitesse 2-litre models had been put on to the market, the first new rear suspension layout had been built in to a car by Ray Henderson's mechanics in the competitions department.

The object, of course, was to provide a new rear wheel geometry, where the massive wheel camber changes present in the existing swing-axle system would be reduced considerably, and to eliminate the tuck-under completely. This could only be done by abandoning the fixed-length swing-axle drive shaft layout, and providing an alternative. The trick would not only be to do this at all (any number of methods would have done a good job), but to achieve it without a major carve-up to existing chassis and body components.

The 'bright idea'—as Harry Webster has dubbed it—was to convert the swing-axle layout to something approaching a double wishbone system, without abandoning the transverse leaf spring. In effect, this was done by making the transverse leaf spring also act as an upper locating arm, or wishbone, with a new lower wishbone tied to the chassis frame and locating the lower end of a new

---

The Vitesse 2-litre Mk 2, for which the original 'bottom wishbone' rear suspension was intended. This car was announced at the same time as the GT6 Mk 2

wheel upright. It was a system which had been used with much success, if not much sophistication, on Cooper Grand Prix cars at the end of the 1950s. One effect of using a rear suspension geometry like this was that there would be variations in the length of the drive shaft between the inner and outer universal joints; some sort of sliding or flexible joint would be needed to accommodate the 'plunge'.

To deal with this, a rubber 'doughnut' was inserted midway along the shaft, or rather between the inner and outer sub-shafts—and sat in the space below the transverse leaf spring, and between the final drive casing, and the rear wheel upright. Not only did this deal with the length variations, but it also provided an excellent shock absorbing cushion between the wheels and the rest of the drive line. In true Standard-Triumph fashion, where no new parts were ever used if existing ones could be pressed into service instead, this doughnut was a lightly modified version of those already in use in the *front* suspension drive shafts of the fwd Triumph 1300.

Their only drawback was that they were rather bulky, but to provide clearance it was simple enough to arrange for the new lower wishbone

castings to be bowed down underneath. There was never a hint of a whirling problem either, for the maximum rotational speed of the doughnut was only of the order of 1800 rpm. It was an interesting detail that the lower wishbone was, in Grand Prix racing parlance, 'reversed', which is to say that there was only a single pivot at the inner (chassis) end, and two pivots at the outer end.

Two other changes made to idealize the set-up were that the alignment of the forward-facing radius arms was changed—the chassis-mounted pick-up points being much nearer to the centre line of the car than before, and there was a new, long and slim, telescopic damper picking up on the inside of the rear body wheelarch, rather than on the chassis frame itself; the GT6 Mk 1 damper layout could not be used as the doughnut got in the way, and this explains why Mk 2 and Mk 3 GT6s have a redundant mounting hole at each side of the rear suspension chassis bridge piece.

The effect on rear suspension geometry was remarkable. Whereas with the original GT6 the total wheel camber change from full bump to full rebound had been no less than 21 degrees, with the

Mk 2 lower-wishbone system it had been reduced to 7 degrees 20 minutes. The height of the rear roll centre had been reduced from 12.8 in. to 6.3 in. (putting it more or less on a par with the height of the front roll centre), and the stiffness of the rear spring had been pushed up by about 15 per cent. At a stroke this converted the GT6 from something of an 'iffy' little machine, especially on low-friction surfaces, to one which could be hurled round corners with the best of the competition.

The suspension, however, was only one new feature ushered in with the Mk 2. The engine, though unchanged in size at 1998 cc, benefitted from the fitment of the new TR5 cylinder head, which was an entirely different casting from that used on previous six-cylinder Triumph engines. Known colloquially as the 'full-width head', it featured different inlet and exhaust ports which threaded their way around the holding down studs, new valves to suit, the TR250 (not TR5) type of cast iron exhaust manifold and light-alloy inlet mani-folding, and a camshaft profile offering not only more overlap (50 degrees instead of 36 degrees around top dead centre) but more lift as well

(0.336 in. instead of 0.312 in.). The cylinder block itself was now completely common with that of the 2498 cc TR5/TR250 casting, which meant that there was no physical reason why the GT6 should not, one day, have been given a similar-sized engine unit. The overall result was that peak power was up from 95 bhp (net) at 5000 rpm, to 104 bhp at

LEFT: *The ingenious 'bottom-wishbone' independent rear suspension applied to the GT6 Mk 2, from autumn 1968. The basic chassis frame needed no modification, though new wishbone pivots were added, and the original damper pivots became redundant. The rubber 'doughnut' in the drive shaft looked after plunge, wind-up, and universal jointing.*

BELOW LEFT: *The rubber 'doughnut' which made the bottom wishbone suspension of the GT6 possible was originally designed for the front-wheel-drive layout of the 1965 Triumph 1300, as this cutaway illustration makes clear*

BELOW: *A well-used GT6, showing off the neat location of the lower-wishbone suspension system*

5300 rpm—an improvement of nearly 10 per cent.

There were no changes to the gearbox or overdrive installation, but for British buyers the 3.27:1 final drive ratio became standard for non-overdrive *and* overdrive transmissions, with 3.89:1 as a 'special order' option. This was not a success, as it meant that the acceleration capability of the 3.89:1/overdrive combination was lost unless the customer insisted on specifying it. Not that the situation was quite as confused (or as clear, if you insist!) in other territories: in North America, for instance, the options had not changed, and you got 3.89:1 with overdrive, and without the choice. Triumph did not, in fact, regularize this final drive ratio situation again until the Mk 3 was launched.

To add to the delights of the suspension change, too, Triumph had been juggling around with the wheels. On the Mk 1 disc wheels had been standard, with a good old traditional British chrome nave plate, while centre-lock wire-spoke wheels had been optional. Except, that is, in the United States, where the wire wheels had been standard. Now, for 1969, there was a new type of disc wheel featuring

dummy and what I can only describe as 'pseudo' Rostyle wheel covers, complete with dummy wheel nuts, which was to be standard for most territories including the USA, though wire-spoke wheels continued to be optional.

There was a new fascia treatment, using matt wood finish to the panel itself, but with TR5-type rocker switches, and a new steering wheel with padded spokes. The heater, which had been an

---

LEFT: *Side view of the 1968/69 GT6 Mk 2, identified by the raised bumpers, dummy Rostyle wheels, and extra air-flow vents in the front wings, and in the rear quarter behind the windows*

BELOW LEFT: *GT6 Mk 2s had a new fascia style, with non-polished wood panel, and face-level air vents from the ventilation system*

BELOW: *Recognition points of a GT6 Mk 2 included the 'bone-in-teeth' front bumper, the badging, the new wheels, and the extra cooling louvres behind the wheel arch cutouts*

optional extra on the Mk 1 (but did anyone ever succeed in buying a GT6 without one?) became standard on the Mk 2, and there were face-level 'eye-ball' vents at each end of the fascia panel to provide fresh air.

There had, in fact, been something of a blitz on the problems of air flow and ventilation, for the bonnet panel now had additional louvres in the side (behind the wheel arch cut-outs), there was a heated rear window element as standard, and there were air outlet grilles in the rear quarter panel, behind the opening rear side window glasses. The other external changes were the use of the raised, 'bone-in-teeth' bumper, in common with that used on the Spitfire Mk 3 since the spring of 1967, and the fitment of a large transverse rear exhaust silencer, which was visible below the tail from the back of the car.

All this, however, had been accompanied by an increase in the car's price. I recall that *Autocar*'s original GT6 road test of September 1967 had ended with the comment that, 'Potentially the GT6 is a fine formula; with further development (and if necessary a price increase) it could become outstanding.', and Triumph had obliged by doing both

of these things. The basic price rose from £800 to £879, with overdrive an extra at £60.70, and wire wheels extra at £38.33.

The GT6 was a much improved little car for 1969, and all the testers loved it, but there was little discernible effect on new-car orders. In 1967 and 1968, 6162 and 6434 GT6s had been built, whereas in 1969 and 1970 (when the Mk 2 was in full flow) these figures changed only marginally, to 6677 and 6474. All of which leads me to ask just how much notice the customer actually takes of published road tests!

Even so, it is worth noting what various magazines had to say. *Road Test*, of North America, wished, 'we had a Celtic gift for words to describe the difference in the way the car behaves on the road. . .', while *Motor*, of Britain headlined their test 'Much Improved' with the added comment that 'New rear suspension greatly improves roadholding and handling'. *Autocar*, who had made the most fuss about the original car, summarised that the 'new rear suspension gives safer, more predictable handling'.

Most of the test cars, incidentally, reached between 107 and 110 mph in a straight line, and

ABOVE: *A careful look at badging tells us that this was a USA-market GT6 Mk 2, known over here as a GT6 Plus. Note, also, the earless centre-lock wheel nuts, and the extra reflectors on the flanks*

ABOVE LEFT: *From the rear, a GT6 Mk 2 made itself clear by the extra air outlet grille in the quarter, and the badging along with the big transverse silencer under the tail*

LEFT: *The padded 'safety' steering wheel of the GT6 Mk 2 actually had the originally sprung spokes hidden away under the padding. The radio was still an extra*

overall fuel consumption figures of about 25/26 mpg (Imperial) were average.

Incidentally, in North America, for marketing reasons which were never clear to us on this side of the Atlantic, the GT6 Mk 2 was renamed GT6+, or GT6 Plus. That was all well and good, but when the time came to launch the GT6 Mk 3 in North America, it was then known as . . . GT6 Mk 3!

At this point I should make clear that North American safety and exhaust emission regulations were already beginning to have an effect on the detail equipment of the GT6, as they had already done on the Spitfire Mk 3. The Mk 2 had different settings to its Zenith-Stromberg carburettors, and high-back 'tombstone' seat squabs. The fascia panel's new rocker-type switches had, of course, been directly inspired by the new regulations.

Customers now began to appreciate owning their new GT6s without having to make excuses for them. Just so long as the little coupés were treated strictly as two seaters, without any attempt being made to squeeze extra passengers into them, the GT6s did a very good and honest job. For a short time, in fact, an 'occasional' (*very* occasional!) rear seat was listed for the Mk 2 (at a price of £19.58), but I have never seen a car with such a seat fitted. It would, in any case, have been almost useless. The space behind the front

The backdrop is Kenilworth castle, and the 1969–70 Triumph sports car line up is on parade. As far as is known, the wheel trims fitted to the GT6 (which is a right-hand drive car) were never fitted, though US-market Spitfires had them for a time

seats, and under the front of the loading platform, was much more useful for stowing valuables out of sight, away from the view of light-fingered car thieves who liked to see what they were stealing before they did the job.

There was no doubt, however, that the GT6 was only just large enough for its marketing slot—one major problem being that it had to face up directly to the MGB GT, which sold for £931 (basic) in 1969 at a time when the GT6 Mk 2 was priced at £979. Although the MGB GT was not as good a car all round (it was slower, thirstier, and heavier to drive) it certainly had more interior space. *Road & Track*, however, summed up the Mk 2's attractions perfectly, 'Where else can you get a 6-cyl, 100+ mph coupé with a proper chassis, good finish and jazzy looks for $3000? Nowhere *we* know of.'

By the time the GT6 Mk 2 went on sale, of course, its future prospects had been affected considerably by the formation of the British Leyland conglomerate. Up to 1968, Triumph had been in direct competition with MG, but now—in theory at least—they had to co-operate in one form or another. In retrospect, it is amazing to recall how British Leyland made no apparent attempt to

rationalize their model range soon after the merger became effective. At the time when economists were predicting the streamlining of the product line, British Leyland actually began to expand theirs.

In 1969, soon after the GT6 Mk 2 had gone into production, Triumph also announced the TR6, which was an extensively face-lifted TR5/TR250, and only a year later, in June 1970, they also revealed their long-rumoured (and considerably delayed) 2 + 2 GT derivative of the Triumph 2000, the V8 engined Stag. By the end of that year, British Leyland were selling no fewer than six different sports cars—the Spitfire, GT6, TR6, Stag, MG Midget/Austin-Healey Sprite, and the MGB—while the six-cylinder MGC had only just gone out of production. All six models were being marketed in North America, where the onslaught of new legislation was becoming more serious every year.

As already recounted, Giovanni Michelotti's proposal for a smart overall re-style of the Spitfire/GT6 bodyshell had had to be modified in the light of new North American legislative rumours, so there could be no question of giving a later version of the GT6 a bonnet with pop-up headlamps. In the interim, therefore, the 1970 model-year GT6 was

given reclining seat backs, a new sporting-style steering wheel, improved cockpit padding, new badging, and matt black windscreen surrounds in place of the previous chrome surround, while hidden away under the skin there were detail structural improvements to make the cars comply with the latest 30 mph barrier crash regulations. As a result of this, the GT6's British basic price rose to £902, which compared with £1080 for the TR6 hardtop model, and £661 for the Spitfire hardtop. It was still nice to know that the MGB GT (also re-touched for 1970) was more expensive, at £970.

While these changes were being phased in (and, at the same time, affected by strike action), GT6 production dropped sharply (to a mere 23 cars in October 1969), but soon recovered to its usual level.

The date in Triumph's archive is February 1968—this being the style being developed by Michelotti and Triumph as a proposal for the GT6 Mk 3/Spitfire Mk IV, but the flip-up headlamp nose was abandoned because of safety legislation fears. What a pity! Note that, at this point, exposed seam bonnets were still being used

I use the word 'usual' advisedly, for once again a definite improvement in specification led to virtually no change in production, or demand: in the spring of 1970, as in 1969, 1968 and 1967, something like 600 cars were built every month.

Even so, British Leyland pressed ahead with the GT6 facelift, in common with that being made to the Spitfire, to turn it into the Mk IV. For no apparent reason (except that it was made clear that the British market was not at all important in terms of the percentage of total sports car sales) the Spitfire Mk IV/GT6 Mk 3 announcement was held back until the end of the Earls Court Motor Show, but it also meant that ample supplies were available in North America at the start of the 1971 season.

Like the Spitfire Mk IV, the GT6 Mk 3 featured a new and smoothed-out bonnet panel, with the wing-top seams now turned inwards, with a more delicate front bumper style, new air inlet grille, and with polycarbonate under-riders. Now there was no sign of cooling louvres in the bonnet—either in the top panel, or the side panels behind the wheel arch cut-outs. The new ventilated disc wheels (no dummy covers were fitted), the deeper windscreen, recessed door handles, and new chopped-off tail were all as standardized for the Mk IV Spitfire, and in this way none of the benefits of panel commonisation were lost.

In the case of the GT6 Mk 3, however, where there was a fixed fastback roof, the opportunity was also taken to reshape that roof towards the tail, and to alter the profile of the rear quarter windows and the air-outlet grilles flanking them.

The actual profile of the wheel arch cut-outs was

BELOW LEFT : *The rear end of Michelotti's proposed (1968) re-style for Spitfires and GT6s was approved, and was launched in the autumn of 1970. This was the GT6 Mk 3, which featured the chopped off tail, the new tail lamps, and the altogether smoother and more integrated detailing*

RIGHT : *As on earlier GT6s, the Mk 3 had its spare wheel and tools packed under the floor of the loading area. The slot in the rear quarter trim is for the outlet ventilation*

BELOW : *The sleek tail of the GT6 Mk 3 included a large lift-up tailgate with (in this case) a heated rear window. The petrol filler cap was flush-mounted on the near side*

marginally different, a degree of flaring being provided to allow wider wheels to be fitted by the owner. Perhaps the neatest modification of all was that the fuel filler cap was now a bright flush-fitting design in the nearside wing, behind the wheel opening, instead of a free-standing cap behind the rear window. The Spitfire's filler, of course, was a centrally-mounted snap-action cap, mounted behind the seats.

Inside the car there was a new steering wheel with polished metal spokes, and the overdrive control was now incorporated in the gear lever knob itself (a Triumph feature introduced first with the Stag model earlier in 1970), while a combined steering lock/ignition switch was specified for the British models for the first time. The rear loading shelf had already been re-shaped to make provision for reclining seats on the 1970-model Mk 2s, this feature being carried forward, while the transmission tunnel was padded to give the occupants even more location (and comfort) during spirited cornering. For the first time there was a slide-type of heater control, though the heater was still of the

water-valve variety, and subject to some testers' criticism.

There seemed to be every chance of the Mk 3 being the most successful GT6 of all, if the dealer and press reaction was to be believed. The original GT6 had sold 15,818 examples, while the Mk 2 had achieved 12,066 cars. There was no proper expla-

LEFT: *The only component Michelotti had not been able to smooth out, or integrate, for the GT6 Mk 3, was the transverse exhaust silencer. The exposed-nut road wheels were like those of the Spitfire Mk IV. Note the re-profiled rear quarter window shape.*

BELOW LEFT: *Smooth Spitfire Mk IV look-alike bonnet (but with a re-profiled engine clearance bulge) was fitted to the GT6 Mk 3, along with different grille and under-rider details. The windscreen was two inches deeper too*

BELOW: *No-one complained about the handling of the GT6 Mk 3, which had the very effective lower-wishbone rear suspension*

BOTTOM: *GT6 Mk 3 engine bay, with 104 bhp engine just like the Mk 2, which featured the latest 'full-width' cylinder head developed originally for the TR5*

BELOW: *Side view of the GT6 Mk 3, where the reprofiled shape of the rear quarter window is most obvious, along with the altered sweep of the tail, the new wheels, air outlets, and recessed door handles*

RIGHT: *Slightly modified Mk 2 fascia style became Mk 3, with a polished wood panel again, and with the overdrive control in the gear lever knob. The steering wheel was also a new design, shared with the Spitfire Mk IV. Note the padding on the gearbox tunnel*

BELOW RIGHT: *The GT6 Mk 3 engine installed, with the air-cleaner overhanging the splash guards, and cold air trunking from the nose of the car to the air-cleaner*

nation, therefore, for the fact that total sales of the Mk 3, in three years, were 13,042 cars! Indeed, monthly production figures never again reached the height of the 1969 and 1970 models, in spite of the fact that the Mk 3 was demonstrably the better car. The shortfall cannot entirely be blamed on poor industrial relations, and the number of strikes occurring at Canley, though it was a dismal fact that there were several of these. In 1971, for example, the launch of Triumph's new Dolomite saloon was put off, not once, but twice, because initial stock build up had been disrupted so much during the summer and autumn.

The fact was, however, that the weight of US legislation was beginning to bear heavily down upon the GT6 model, and sales sank steadily away. More than 13,000 Mk 1s had been exported (mostly to North America), but less than 11,000 Mk 2s had made the same currency-earning journeys, and the number fell again for the Mk 3.

Exhaust emission regulations affected the six-cylinder engine badly, and in spite of the man-power (and man-hours) which Triumph threw into the battle, and power outputs gradually and inexorably fell away. The British and European peak figure of 104 bhp (net) was never matched for the USA. 95 bhp was available in 1969 and 1970, 90 bhp in 1971, and a mere 79 bhp (net, at 4900 rpm) was on offer for 1972 and 1973. It was all very depressing.

Even in Britain the quoted maximum power output crept slowly downwards. In 1971 *Autocar*'s test car had 98 bhp (net) at 5300 rpm, while in 1972 (unannounced) it had been further reduced to 95 bhp (net) at 5250 rpm. The plain truth was that the engine, designed in the 1950s, and extensively re-developed in the mid-1960s, was rapidly running out of development potential; even in 2498 cc form, in the TR6, it was struggling. By the early 1970s, in

Everything open on the GT6 Mk 3—this is a 'federal' example, destined for the USA

fact, Triumph had started to design a new engine to replace it, though this was not expected to be ready until 1975 at least; the unit eventually found its way into the Rover SD1 2300/2600 models, and does not appear ever to have been run in two-litre guise.

On top of the engine power restrictions there was the impact of safety legislation, which ensured that more and yet more strengthening devices had to be added to the chassis and body, that weight crept inexorably upwards, and that the car became more costly to build and sell. It was the sort of situation businessmen hate to face—they were having to put up their prices without ostensibly improving the product, and they *knew* the customers were increasingly unhappy about the situation. That, and the GT6's in-house competition for favour with no fewer than five other British Leyland products in North America, all made it vulnerable.

That did not deflect the magazine testers' views, that the GT6 Mk 3 was now a thoroughly good little car. *Autocar* dubbed it a 'Close-fitting fun car', and said that the recent changes had produced 'a much

smoother, more coherent design'. Their car, incidentally, was faster than any previous GT6, with a top speed of 112 mph in the 3.27 : 1 direct top gear—there was no overdrive on the test car. Even more remarkable, perhaps, was the 96 mph (at 6000 rpm) recorded in third gear, and the 68 mph possible in second gear. *Wheels* of Australia called it a 'taut, stubby little roadster you grab and fling around just for the sheer fun of it'. Even *Motor Sport*, usually crotchety enough to give any PR man palpitations at the thought of what they might say about his car, called the Mk 3 'Good Value from British Leyland' and went on to say that 'for someone who still likes the idea of a two-seater with excellent yet unfussy performance complete with all the mod cons of a well-finished interior, wind-down windows and so

Consider the effect of this 150 bhp 2498 cc version of the Triumph six-cylinder engine, in a GT6 Mk 2 or Mk 3 chassis . . . It could have been made to fit, too, fuel injection and all

on there isn't much to beat the GT6'. Even *Car*, whose staff offer didn't seem to enthuse over *any* car unless it was Italian, thought the GT6 had 'a certain charm, due mainly to its compact build and handling qualities.'

Time was running out for the GT6, but there was still time for one more revision. Announced in February 1973, to coincide with changes also being made to the TR6 and the Spitfire Mk IV for North America, the GT6 not only got restyled instruments, strengthened bumper mountings, a smaller steering wheel and fire-retarding trim and upholstery, but it also lost its lower-wishbone rear suspension!

The rear suspension change was not as drastic as might have been feared, and there was to be no going back to the bad old days of the swing-axle horrors of 1966–8. Instead the GT6 was commonized with the 1973-model Spitfire, which is to say that it inherited the swing-spring layout, but that it also had a wider rear track. No road test cars to this specification were ever issued for appraisal, but a drive in a 1973-model GT6 years later shows that the handling was only imperceptibly (if at all) inferior to that of the 'lower-wishbone' car. British Leyland never tried to justify the change as an improvement (which it was not), and the reason was almost certainly on the grounds of cost reduction.

At the same time, for Europe and Great Britain, a vacuum servo was added to the breaking system,

and Sundym tinted glass was standardized. By this time the weight had crept up to 2020 lb., about 115 lb. more than that of the original Mk 1 of 1966. Documents preserved by the factory show that a change from Laycock D-type to the new J-type overdrive were proposed for 1974, but all GT6 owners know that this never happened, as the car was withdrawn from production at the end of 1973. The weight of legislation in the United States had finally got the better of the GT6, and it can have been no consolation to followers of this fine little car to see that the Stag was also withdrawn from North America at the same time. British Leyland's retrenchment had indeed begun, for their new V8-engined MGB GT was never to be put on sale in North America at all, while the four-cylinder MGB GT itself was withdrawn at the end of 1974.

Only 4218 of the swing-spring 1973-model GT6s were ever built, and the last were assembled before the end of the year. It was a slow, lingering, death, with 34 cars rolling off the lines in the last two weeks

---

LEFT: *The year is 1972, and this is the complete line-up of contemporary Triumph sports models. Top to bottom: Spitfire Mk IV, GT6 Mk 3, TR6, Stag, and Dolomite saloon*

BELOW: *Could this fast-back Stag hatchback have displaced the GT6? Perhaps it could—but only the one prototype was built*

of October 1973, two more in mid-November, and the last two at the very end of that month. British Leyland made no announcement—they just allowed the car gently to fade away.

So how does the GT6 measure up, in historical terms? Statistically, there were 40,926 cars of three distinct varieties, and about 80 per cent were exported. When you compare this with other British Leyland sporting cars of the period—a total of 2591 MGB GT V8s sold, for instance, and a seven-year Stag output of 25,877, the GT6's achievement (and success) falls into place.

It was a success, and while the lines were full of other Herald/Vitesse/Spitfire derivatives it must also have been a good profitmaker for the group. Perhaps it would have been a better car, and more warmly received, if it had been a few inches longer in the wheelbase, rather wider, and more distinctively styled—but then that was never possible. To expect the GT6 to have been anything other than what it was is to miss the whole point of the exercise. By skilfully shuffling existing components, and by mixing in a dash of flair, Triumph produced a new model at minimum expense. It was a great credit to Harry Webster's engineers, and to the 'can-do' spirit which prevailed at Coventry in those years. It is only now, some years after production ceased for ever, that the GT6's true worth is being realized.

The GT6's 'Big Brother'—the 3-litre vee-8-engined Stag, with 2 + 2 seating and a permanent T-bar rollover safety feature

Facts and figures: GT6 Mk 2

Built July 1968 to December 1970
Number built 12,066
Chassis numbers KC50001 to KC58046 inclusive. Then, from October 1969, KC75001 to KC82398 inclusive.

Engine 6-cyl, in-line, cast-iron cylinder block and cylinder head, with four crankshaft main bearings. Bore, stroke and capacity, 74.7 × 76 mm., 1998 cc (2.94 × 2.99 in., 122 cu. in.). CR 9.25:1, 2 Zenith-Stromberg carburettors. 104 bhp (net) at 5300 rpm. Maximum torque 117 lb. ft at 3000 rpm.

Transmission Final drive 3.27:1. Overall gear ratios 3.27, 4.11, 5.82, 8.66, reverse 10.13:1. Optional overdrive with 3.27:1 final drive ratio, overall o/d ratio 2.62:1. Later cars with optional overdrive had 3.89:1 final drive ratio, and overall ratios of (o/d 3.11), 3.89, 4.86, 6.92, 10.30, reverse 12.06:1. Synchromesh on all forward gears. Overdrive (optional) on top and third gears. 20.1 mph/1000 rpm in direct top gear with overdrive not fitted; 25.2 mph/1000 rpm in overdrive top (3.27:1 final drive); 21.2 mph/1000 rpm in overdrive top (3.89:1 final drive).

Basic prices UK £879 at first, £902 from October 1969 (start-up of 1970 model), £925 from February 1970
USA $2995 (1969), $3095 (1970).

Suspension and brakes 9.7 in. front disc brakes, 8 × 1.25 in. rear drums. 155-13 in. radial ply tyres on 4.5 in. rim bolt-on steel disc wheels, or centre-lock wire-spoke wheels. Independent rear suspension by transverse leaf spring and lower wishbones.

Dimensions Length 12 ft 1 in.; width 4 ft 9 in.; height 3 ft 11 in. Front track 4 ft 1 in.; rear track 4 ft 1 in. Unladen weight 1904 lb.

Facts and figures: GT6 Mk 3

Built October 1970 to December 1973
Number built 13,042
Chassis numbers KE1 onwards (1971), KE10001 onwards (1972). From February 1973, KE20001 to KE24218 inclusive. (KF prefix for US-market cars, 1972 and 1973).

General The GT6 Mk 3 had a completely re-skinned body style (based on that of the Spitfire Mk IV) with seamless bonnet, cut-off 'corporate-style' tail, and other details.

Technical specification as for GT6 Mk 2 except for:
Transmission Final drive ratios as final GT6 Mk 2 (and original GT6 Mk 1)—3.27:1 without overdrive, 3.89:1 with overdrive. Reverse gear ratio 9.85:1 without overdrive fitted, 11.71:1 with overdrive fitted.

Basic prices UK £970 at first, rising persistently to £1285 by end of 1973
USA $3374 (1971), $3523 (1972), $3955 (1973), $4350 (1974)

Suspension and brakes Independent rear suspension by transverse leaf spring and lower wishbones at first; from February 1973, by swing axles and pivoting-spring leaf spring location.

Dimensions Length 12 ft 5 in. Front track 4 ft 1 in.; rear track 4 ft 1 in. to end 1972; from February 1973 rear track 4 ft 2 in. Unladen weight 2030 lb.

Chapter 8

Triumphant abroad:
American export success

In 1978, 30 members of the US-based Vintage Triumph Register visited the Coventry works, where they were entertained by then managing director Jeff Herbert. 'I am pleased to advise,' he told them over coffee, 'that the Triumph Spitfire will continue in production.'

You could have heard the cheering in Hoboken.

For people who delighted in pre-1970 Triumphs, this was an interesting expression of support. For them it was not so much that the Spitfire was a good car, although it was that. What VTR people saw was rather a symbol: the last throwback to the glory days of the Triumphs they themselves owned—back even to the last TR3s, which were sold alongside the first Spitfires.

It was hard to believe that the Spitfire had been around since 1963; that it had sold, by then, about 120,000 units in the United States alone. Jeff Herbert's lease on life gave the car yet two more years of production. Thus the final record: 18 years, one of the longest spans for any sports car and twice that of the longest-running TR; over a quarter million units of which 75 per cent were exported, nearly two-thirds of those going to the USA.

The Spitfire accomplished these impressive feats in the face of formidable competition by the lower priced Austin-Healey Sprite and its badge-engineered, ultimate successor, the MG Midget. This rivalry continued even after the BMH-Leyland merger in 1968, ultimately involving quite serious MG-Triumph dealer confrontations. But the Spitfire met its competition squarely. Despite its higher price—always a few dollars (in the 1970s several hundred dollars) more expensive than the Spridgets, it was nevertheless a real volume seller. In 1965 it broke 9000 in US sales. If the Sprite or Midget are considered separately, neither matched Spitfire's US sales. Indeed the 18-year US total almost equalled those of the Sprite and Midget

combined. Had BL kept it in full production through 1981, Spitfire volume would probably have surpassed that of its former foes.

Back in 1963, though such successes weren't certain, they were definite possibilities. Standard-Triumph had planned well: the Spitfire was very carefully targeted to the USA with a neat design, a sophisticated spec. and a strong factory-backed competition programme, all laid down before its introduction. And they all came together—with a little bit of luck.

When what S-T/USA called the 'Spitfire 4' made its debut at the Miami Auto Show in January 1963, it caused an immediate sensation. Though more expensive than the Sprite, if offered much more for the money. Good looks, for example. While the Mark I frog-eye Sprite had won adherents by its sheer friendly-ugliness, the then-current Mark II simply looked ordinary. Spitfire's Michelotti styling, with swoopy wings, dipped beltline and pert tail, was more appealing to style-conscious Yanks. Mechanically the Spitfire offered an independent rear end—albeit via swing axles—against the Sprite's conventional beam; it had a larger engine, for better acceleration and less buzziness at speed. But its greatest advantage was comfort: There was more interior and boot space in virtually every direction and, praise be, there were even roll-up windows.

Even the name was right. To Americans, *Spitfire* was less sacred than to Britons—it meant, not a classic fighter aircraft, but a devil-may-care pinto pony, or a high-spirited girl from 'Somewhere West

Until amalgamated within British Leyland's North American organisation, Standard-Triumph had their own headquarters—this was their final home, at Teaneck, New Jersey

of Laramie.' The label was ideal. And so, at $475 below the Triumph TR4, was the price.

'In the early days, of course, the Spitfire was exactly what Triumph dealers needed,' said Graham Whitehead, president of Jaguar-Rover-Triumph Inc. in New Jersey. 'The price structure was spot-on.' Just as the TR4 led the MGB just slightly in price, the Spitfire 4 led the Sprite/Midget combine, and the dollar difference was enough to allow the above-mentioned advantage. Triumph had taken a look at the BMC offerings, found them lacking, and had paid attention to improving the same concept of a low-bucks sports car.

Why would an American be willing to pay $200 more for, say, a 1968 Mk 3 Spitfire than a 1968 Sprite? This is a good year to examine, as it was the first time the two rivals were comparison-tested by an American magazine, *Road & Track*. (The Midget must be disregarded, because in 1968 its base price was only $20 less than Spitfire's!)

Compared to the Spitfire, the Sprite was a somewhat dated design, *R & T* noted. Indeed, it was five years older. It was smaller and lighter, if well-built and rattle-free. *R & T* drivers ranked the Sprite's handling superior compared to the wild tuck-under of the Spitfire rear end, the Sprite cornered as if on rails, with moderate roll oversteer that was easily controlled. But handling was where the Sprite advantages stopped. Its tiny cockpit, *R & T* noted, 'automatically eliminated the 6 ft-or-over driver. The seat won't go back far enough . . .

the pedals are too small and too close . . . the steering wheel is too close . . . the doors are small enough to make it difficult to get in or out, as well as having such a high windowsill.'

The Spitfire, by contrast, rated 'very good so far as driving position and comfort are concerned. The steering wheel is well placed, the seats are comfortable, the controls are where they should be and so on. The H-pattern of the 4-speed shift is slightly skewed but one quickly acclimates to this.' And of course the Spitfire buried the Sprite when it came to interior space and luggage capacity. In performance, the comparison was also in Spitfire's favour:

	Spitfire	Sprite
0–30 mph, sec.	4.1	4.3
0–60 mph, sec.	13.6	14.7
0–70 mph, sec.	22.6	25.6
Top speed, mph	100	93

Even the peculiar characteristics of the swing-axle rear suspension, *R & T* noted, were not a serious shortcoming for the experienced driver: 'From the driver's seat it is somewhat less disturbing as you feel the body twitch over . . . what you have to do is feather the throttle, juggle the steering wheel to flatten it out again and then continue to balance yourself and the car on this tightrope through the bend.' The editors noted that an aftermarket supplier offered a $25 camber compensator 'that will do more good for the Spitfire's handling. Some decambering also is possible and will be desirable.

The Leyland-BMH merger of January 1968 presented US dealers with a 'whole new ballgame'. Out of the blue, rivals of the past five years were to become linemates—or so British Leyland hoped. 'There wasn't much resistance from either MG or Triumph dealers to taking on an opposite line,' said Michael L. Cook, public relations manager for Jaguar-Rover-Triumph, and at that time a staffman of the Triumph organization. 'Most of them looked upon the merger as a good thing, in that it added to their saleable lines. We had different

---

RIGHT: *Graham Whitehead, President of British Leyland Motors Inc., of North America, for many years, posing with a specially 'Spitfire' decal'd Mk 3 at the New York show in 1970*

BELOW RIGHT: *The Spitfire was a '1500' in North America well before it became available in the rest of the world. This was a 1974 version with unique badging (abandoned, for 1975, with transfers), and the new front spoiler*

BELOW: *The original US-market Spitfire of 1963 looked much like the domestic version, except that special wheel trims were standardised*

techniques for doubling and rationalizing the various franchises. In Canada, the company merely announced that all BLMC products would be made available to all previous BMH or Triumph dealers, period. They could refuse a line if they wanted, but in practice, few did. In California, our distributor set out to dual as many agencies as possible, and he was successful.

'There were few dealer rivalries in 1968,' Cook continued, 'but rather more later on.' When US automotive sales began to slip following the Arab oil boycott of 1973–4, specialty manufacturers like BL were particularly hard-hit. 'The situation would occur of a former Triumph dealer trying to take over from the former BMH dealer down the street and vice versa,' Cook recalled, 'each knowing that dealer bodies would be reduced and confined. This was a very real problem.'

Turning to the merger of the two managerial organizations, Cook said there was little difficulty: 'For five years after the merger, separate sales organizations continued. Bruce McWilliams, for example, was vice-president of Triumph and Land Rover sales, and he had come into the BLMC organisation from Standard-Triumph. In 1973 Mike Dale became VP for all sales and Bruce moved

to president of product planning. It worked very smoothly. The physical plants were easily merged. In late 1968 the entire operation was concentrated at our new building in Leonia, New Jersey; Standard-Triumph moved there from smaller quarters in Teaneck, which it had occupied since May 1966.' (The Leonia building is still the headquarters of BL in the United States.)

'If there was any place where rivalries between former Leyland and BMH people caused us trouble, I would say it was the factories,' Cook continued. 'Here there were many problems for BL-USA, for example in safety and emissions testing. Too much was spent doing things in parallel—in Coventry for Triumph, in Abingdon for MG.'

Federal regulation of the American auto industry—and, by definition, every car imported as well—began with the passage of the Clean Air and Highway Safety Acts during the administration of President Johnson. Though the manufacturers had been showing a willingness to voluntarily improve safety—switching to amber turn signals in 1963, standardizing seat belt anchor points and later seat belts themselves—this was not considered enough for the 'Great Society.' Compulsion was selected over voluntarism. The first wave of Federal re-

gulations came in 1968, and with them the Spitfire was forced to comply or retire. Thus arrived Mark 3, the first Spitfire with separate specifications for the USA market. Though both versions of the Mark 3 were more powerful than their predecessor, the European car produced 75 bhp on 9:1 compression, while the US version offered only 68 bhp on 8.5:1. The USA Mark IV (1971–4) was detuned to 58 bhp, and the final Spitfire 1500 (1975–81) dropped to 57 bhp despite a gain of 200 cc. These changes, to neutralize what few emissions a 1.5 litre four spewed into the atmosphere, were made at the sacrifice of considerable performance. Contrast for example, the following figures published in a 1976 comparison test with the 1968 figures earlier noted:

	Spitfire 1500/USA	Spitfire 1500/GB*
0–30 mph, sec.	4.8	3.8
0–60 mph, sec.	15.3	13.2
0–70 mph, sec.	22.3	18.1
Top speed, mph	94	100
Mpg (US gal.)	25.0	36.5

*Autocar tested 3/75

Despite what they did to fuel economy, Federal regulations did cause certain beneficial changes to be made in the US specification—albeit at a price, which contributed to the Spitfire's soaring inflation during the middle and late 1970s. The later Mark 3 met government mandates with a new matt-finished dash replacing the glossy fascia, in which all instruments were black-bezelled and placed squarely in front of the driver. Two-speed wipers, a high-impact laminated windscreen, rocker-type electrical switches, and a centre-mounted, illuminated control panel for the heater/demister unit were also provided to meet Federal statutes. The Mark 3

ALL: *The way in which minor development, and decorative changes were made to North American Spitfires—a 1975 1500 with built in licence plate holder, a 1976 1500 with blacked-up wiper arms, different wheel style, and British Leyland decal, and—finally—the 1980 model with the 'safety' rear bumpers (black colour for the only time in the car's 18-year life), energy absorbing black front bumper and overriders, a different spoiler, and check-pattern seat facings and a fixed door mirror*

Spitfire also adopted the infamous 'bone in the teeth' raised front bumper to meet Federal minimum height requirements. Even more unfortunate, for those not subject to such laws, Triumph elected to cut costs by building all of them that way. Thus Mark 3 for every market wore this ugly badge of engineering-by-politician.

The US Mark IV Spitfire, which appeared at the New York Auto Show in 1971, carried the same high bumper with a pair of large rubber pads substituting for overriders to meet minimum crash standards. On the plus side, Triumph redesigned the rear style along Stag lines, with a smooth, flat, chrome-edged boot tapering to a flat panel neatly carrying the number plate and taillamps.

The would-be Mark V was dubbed Spitfire 1500, and once again was created primarily to keep up with Federal requirements. Changes made either in compliance with mandates or in anticipation of

GT6 introduction, at the Triumph showrooms in New York City, 1967

same included inertia-reel seatbelts in 1973, rheostat instrument panel lighting in 1974, steering-column located ignition/washer/wiper/horn/light controls in 1977, and an ugly all-black bumper of ponderous proportions in 1980. Laycock overdrive was retained as a US option through the end of production, and press releases made much of its ability to improve fuel mileage from the mid-Seventies on. The US Environmental Protection Agency, which began testing cars for fuel mileage in 1973, quoted a highway average of 32 US mpg, (35 with overdrive) (40/43.8 Imperial) for the 1978–80 Spitfire, for example. But in the real world, the figures were more like 22/25 US (27.5/31.3 Imperial). Interestingly, after 1979 the Spitfire could not be sold in California, whose emissions laws had progressed beyond the capacity of engineers to meet without sacrificing what remained of the car's performance.

When BMH and Leyland merged in 1968, they had to consider the role not only of Spitfire versus Spridget, but that of their recently announced grand touring cars, the Triumph GT6 and the MGB GT. This proved, however, a less distressing

problem. While the open cars were aggressive rivals by design, noted Mike Cook 'The GT6 and the MGB were really very different cars. If anything, the dealers were even happier to have both of them to sell than the two open sports models.' But in the end this difference told against the GT6. 'Its main problem from a US sales standpoint was its size,' Cook continued. 'It was so very small—to the eye it looked even smaller than the Spitfire. Had there been some design evolution—a higher roofline, a wider track, and the resulting increase in interior space—it would have proved much more saleable.'

On introduction in 1967, the GT6 was the fastest car in the USA Triumph range—marginally quicker than even the TR4A. More to the point— for they were still rivals at that time—it was quicker *and cheaper* than the MGB GT. Its smooth, two-litre six was worlds happier on American highways than MG's buzzy 1.8 litre four. It's strange that no prominent US magazine made an early comparison of the two cars; indeed the Spitfire was more often compared to the Jaguar E type coupé than the MGB GT. But the figures are worth quoting in any book devoted to Triumphs:

	1967 GT6 o/d (R & T **4/67**)	1966 MGB GT (R & T **5/66**)
0–30 mph, sec.	4.4	4.0
0–60 mph, sec.	12.3	13.6
0–70 mph, sec.	16.4	18.3
0–90 mph, sec.	31.9	37.2
Top speed, mph	107	107
Mpg, (US/Imp.)	24/30	23/29

While it must be granted that the GT6 was fitted with optional Laycock overdrive, which offered certain shifting advantages over the non-O/D MGB GT, the axle ratios of both cars in direct top were nearly identical. And at steady high speeds, which was what these cars were supposed to do best, the GT6's noise level was lower.

There was however one point in which the MGB GT scored: design. While the original GT6 looked pretty good—aggressive even, with that big hood bulge, the later Mark 3 (1971–3) deteriorated with the ugly raised bumper-cum-rubber pads, while the MGB GT was a timeless design which survived the Federal 'bumperising' in better fettle. What's more, the BGT had decent room inside, whereas the GT6 was unsuitable for anyone over six feet tall.

Apparently, the number of six foot Americans and their craving for space to move around in was a greater factor than traditional Yankee preference for big, easy revving engines—at least when it came

to sports cars. Though the GT6 closely matched the BGT's sales in 1968–9, the MG began pulling away in 1970, ultimately sold nearly twice as many units in the USA, and lasted a year longer.

In 1971, shortly before the MGB grew its 'Federal face', *Road & Track* got around to comparing the two cars, along with three other rivals in a now-very-full field: the Datsun 240Z, Fiat 124 Sport and Opel GT. Stylewise *R & T* found the GT6's new rear end better, though they cannily noted that it bore more than a passing resemblance to the old Sunbeam Harrington Le Mans. It still scored ahead of the MGB GT in performance:

	1971 GT6	1971 MGB GT
0–60 mph, sec.	12.0	13.6
$\frac{1}{4}$-mile, sec/mph	18.6/74.5	19.6/72.0
Top speed, mph	107	105
Mpg, US/Imp	23.2/29.0	24.1/30.0

A more significant point, however, is that both British cars were rated distinctly inferior to their oriental and continental rivals, the 240Z leading the pack by a long way. Bear in mind that in those days you could buy any one of these cars for about $3500—and at that figure the Datsun was an incredible bargain. But the Fiat and Opel also had the legs of the British cars in handling, ergonomics, quality of assembly, and general professionalism of the interior and exterior layouts. It had become apparent to the editors, as to most American buyers by that time, that British Leyland was letting its two grand touring cars wither on the vine—to sell as long as there were customers, and to go out of production after that.

'Though the GT6 scores aesthetically and in performance over the MGB, it loses it all on comfort,' *R & T* summarized. 'Its seating is the most cramped in the group, the steering wheel is very high, and its seatbelts were next to impossible to adjust to fit anybody. Triumph has gone to greater lengths to update the GT6 than MG has the B, but it still failed to make much of an impression . . . we do not wish to kick dead horses and sincerely hope that England will be able to get off her duff, produce some competitive cars again and challenge the other countries.' The editors then predicted 'a medium price GT replacing both the B and the GT6—one that we hope will render the choice of a good $3500 GT a bit more difficult to make.'

Alas *Road & Track*, and a whole generation of MG and Triumph enthusiasts, were to be disappointed. GT6 sales in America never surpassed 3000 units from 1971, and the last leftover '73s were gone by mid-1974. The BGT kept on slogging at reduced sales levels through 1975 when it, too, disappeared. No replacement for either car ever came close to production. And it was a shame. Leyland had in both these cars—but the GT6 in particular—the basis of a fine GT for the 1980s. The opportunity was there, too, because the Datsun was soon to grow fat, the Opel GT was to disappear, as was the Fiat 124 Sport.

We asked Mike Cook if the Spitfire and GT6 were dropped because they were unprofitable. His answer, 'Never. They always made money. BL never rated them unprofitable on the world level, as it did the MGB and the TR7/8. They were a 'hard sell' the last few years, of course—I recall that the

last GT6s listed for $4350, which is a lot to pay for a $2895 automobile—and they went out with a $750 or $1000 rebate.'

Press hard enough, and you can even get the devoted Mr Cook to admit that the USA Spitfire/GT6 story in the late 1970s was one of missed opportunities. The Spitfire/Spridget and the GT6/MGB GT ended their days as reluctant partners within a greatly rationalised Leyland-USA range. Very possibly the fact that they were no longer built by competitors was a barrier to new and better evolutions.

The stay-of-execution pronounced to VTR members that day in 1978 was mainly due to the American dealers, who by then were taking 90 per cent of Spitfire production. 'The dealers wanted it in,' Cook recalled. 'For our part, at BL/USA, we were nervous about losing a model. What was left that could fill the gap? In the short term we could have gone on selling 9000 Spitfires a year—but only in the short term. Ultimately they would have had to give us a new car. And they never did.'

RIGHT: *American style TV promotion was aggresive for the whole Triumph range*

BELOW: *Bruce McWilliams (left) and driver Bob Tullius, with the Quaker-State Group 44 GT6+ in 1969*

Hop on the Triumph band wagon.

Use color TV to sell Triumph. This great new commercial is available FREE as a 20 or 60-second spot. Schedule your spots NOW. Order film from Mike Cook, Standard-Triumph Motor Co., Inc., 111 Galway Place, Teaneck, N.J. 07666

ANNCR (VO):
This is the new Triumph GT-6.

And if you think it's just another fastback—
—you're wrong!

It's the new fastback that's also a true sports car.

With big six-cylinder power.

Four-speed stick shift.

Disc brakes.

Bucket seats.

And the tight cornering,

quick steering feeling . . .

you get only with a genuine sports car.

The Triumph GT-6 Fastback looks like . . .

drives like a true sports car . . .

because it is!

People tell us . . .

it's the car that sells itself!

See the new Triumph GT-6 Fastback at your Triumph dealer.

You'll find it alongside the Triumph Spitfire . . .

2000 sedan . . .

and TR-4A.

See the Yellow Pages for your nearest Triumph Dealer.

159

Technically speaking ... the Spitfire in the United States

At first, USA-specification Spitfires were virtually identical with home-market models. Once exhaust emission and safety legislation began to affect the design, however, USA-specification models began to

differ considerably. Compared with UK home-market models, therefore, USA-specification Spitfires differed as follows:

1963 to 1968 models	Virtually the same	
1969 Mk 3 model	CR 8.5:1 68 bhp (net) at 5500 rpm	73 lb. ft at 3000 rpm Unladen weight 1652 lb.
1970 Mk 3 model	CR 9.0:1 Single Zenith-Stromberg carburettor 68 bhp (net) at 5500 rpm	73 lb. ft at 3000 rpm Unladen weight 1652 lb.
1971 Mk IV model	CR 9.0:1 Single Zenith-Stromberg carburettor	58 bhp (net) at 5200 rpm 72 lb. ft at 3000 rpm
1972 Mk IV model	CR 8.0:1 Single Zenith-Stromberg carburettor	48 bhp (net) at 5500 rpm 61 lb. ft at 2900 rpm

1972 Mk IV model: Final drive ratio 4.11:1. Overall gear ratios 4.11, 5.71, 8.87, 14.40, reverse 16.39:1. Optional overdrive, 3.29:1. 15.9 mph/1000 rpm in direct top gear; 19.9 mph/1000 rpm in overdrive top gear.

1973 Mk IV model (Called 1500) 1500 engine used (not adopted by UK-market until 1975). CR 7.5:1 Single Zenith-Stromberg carburettor. 57 bhp (net) at 5000 rpm. Transmission as UK model (3.89:1 final drive). 74 lb. ft at 3000 rpm

1974 Mk IV model (Called 1500) As for 1973 USA-specification model, and incorporating 155-13 in. radial ply tyres.

1975 1500 model As 1974 USA-specification model, but with air-pump and exhaust emission recirculating exhaust system (plus catalyst for California). Unladen weight 1828 lb.

1976 1500 model Power outputs no longer officially quoted. Compression ratio 9.0:1 (not for California).

1977 1500 model Compression ratio 7.5:1, all models, and catalyst fitted, all models.

1978 1500 model Unladen weight now 1850 lb.

1979 1500 model Energy absorbing bumpers fitted to front and rear for first time. Overall length 13 ft 1.5 in.

1980 1500 model Unladen weight now 1875 lb. Spitfire no longer available in California.

Technically speaking ... the GT6 in the United States

GT6s sent to the United States differed from UK- and no 1974 model-year USA derivative existed.

1967 and 1968 Mk 1 models—virtually the same

1969 and 1970 Mk 2 models were known as 'GT6+'. Optional overdrive came with the 3.89:1 final drive ratio. Due to engine 'exhaust emission' limitations, maximum power and torque were:
95 bhp (net) at 4700 rpm
117 lb. ft at 3400 rpm

1971 to 1973 Mk 3 models reverted to normal 'Mk 3' model names. Due to engine 'exhaust emission' limitations, engine specifications were as follows:

1971	CR 9.25:1	90 bhp (net) at 4700 rpm 116 lb. ft at 3400 rpm
1972	CR 8.0:1	79 bhp (net) at 4900 rpm 97 lb. ft at 2900 rpm
1973	CR 8.0:1	79 bhp (net) at 4900 rpm 97 lb. ft at 2900 rpm

Production of the GT6 came to end in December 1973, and no 1974 model-year USA derivative existed

USA selling prices—Spitfire, GT6 and rivals

All prices in $US, POE East Coast

Year	Spitfire	Austin-Healey Sprite	MG Midget	GT6	MGB GT
1963	2199	1875	1945		
1964	2199	1875	1945		
1965	2199	1925	2095		
1966	2155	1888	2055		
1967	2199	1995	2174		3095
1968	2235	2050	2215	2895	3160
1969	2295	2081	2252	2995	3202
1970	2395	2081	2279	3095	3260
1971	2649		2395	3374	3495
1972	2699		2520	3523	3615
1973	2995		2795	3955	4070
1974	3345		3095	4350	4495
1975	3745		3549		4649
1976	4295		3949		
1977	4500		4150		
1978	5350		4850		
1979	5795		5200		
1980	5995				
1981	6250				

USA sales—Spitfire, GT6 and rivals

All sales by calendar year

Year	Spitfire	Austin-Healey Sprite	MG Midget	GT6	MGB GT
1963	6224	5343	3517		
1964	8761	5755	4363		
1965	9097	5198	5561		
1966	6782	5379	3838		
1967	5643	4793	3505	2000	5031
1968	5711	4759	3556	4302	4382
1969	6240	6255	4730	4254	4765
1970	6305	1766	10895	4066	6036
1971	8266		10683	2970	5305
1972	9687		12154	2753	3727
1973	7796		11652	2198	3398
1974	7373		8962	115	3093
1975	8857		9048		2081
1976	6846		11219		
1977	9463		11892		
1978	10231		9385		
1979	8344		9165		
1980	4037		1902[2]		
1981	3924[1]		284[2]		
Total	139,547	39,248	136,310	22,658	37,818

[1] January–August, leftover 1980 models
[2] 1980 and 1981—leftover 1979 models

Chapter 9
Spitfire 1500: last and best?

Sometimes, in the motor industry, it takes ages for a 'good idea' to be developed, refined, and put on to the market. In the case of the final enlargement of the Standard-Triumph SC engine, to 1493 cc, Harry Webster had the 'good idea' at the end of the 1950s, but prototype engines were not built until 1965, and the engine was not actually put on sale in Britain until mid-1970. Spitfire owners had to wait even longer—until the beginning of the 1973 model-year.

I should make it clearer still; there was also a further two-year wait *outside* North America, before the 1493 cc engine became generally available in all Spitfires. I doubt if Triumph, and British Leyland, truly wanted to bring the engine into service as early as they did, but the onslaught of exhaust emission regulations made it essential.

But what about the engine itself? To analyse its development, I ought to go back to the origins of the design—the SC engine of the early 1950s. It has been clarified to me on several occasions that the SC was never specifically designed to incorporate a lot of 'stretch' for the future. In the early and mid-1950s it was meant to be built as 803 cc or 948 cc, and that was that. The need to make the developing Herald family more powerful, and to allow a six-cylinder version of the design to be enlarged to a full 2-litres, encouraged Harry Webster, Jim Parkinson, and their design staffs to look for ways of enlarging an engine which was popularly supposed to have reached its limit.

As I have already detailed in earlier chapters, it was the re-shuffle of bore centres, at the beginning of the 1960s, which made further enlargement possible without the original 'benchmark' stroke of 76 mm having to be changed. By 1963 the 1296 cc four-cylinder engine had been developed for the front wheel-drive 1300 (and later for the Spitfire), while the six-cylinder engine was being built as 1596 cc or

1998 cc. Both engines were at the limit of their capacities with the standard 76 mm stroke—the four-cylinder unit having a bore of 73.7 mm, and the 'six' a bore of 74.7 mm.

In almost every Triumph model, however, there was a need for more power and torque, to keep up with the opposition—for the 1950s and 1960s was a period when most manufacturers concentrated on making their cars faster, rather than safer and more economical. Triumph, having gone through the period of near-bankruptcy in the 1060–2 period, had no new power units in the pipe-line, for such items would have been ruinously expensive to tool up and prepare for production.

Under Leyland's ownership, and with a welcome and stable return to profitability from 1963 onwards, two decisions were taken. One was to set about the design of all new engines of one family, to cover the 1.3-litre to 3.0-litre range, and the other was to achieve a final stretch of existing overhead-valve designs. The bare bones of the new family of engines was sketched out in a masterly series of confidential papers called *A study of Engine Design for the Late 1960s and 1970s*, which were to the credit of Lewis Dawtrey—this family eventually matured as the single-overhead-camshaft slant-4 and V8 engines fitted to cars like the Dolomite, the TR7, and the Stag, though none ever found a place in the Spitfire/GT6 family.

These new engines could not possibly be made ready, it was reasoned, before the end of the 1960s, and an interim solution to the 'power race' problem

Compared with Mk IVs, the Spitfire 1500s looked almost identical. The head restraints had been standard on USA model cars for years, and were fitted to UK-market cars from the start of 1973

was needed at once. Standard-Triumph therefore set about finding a way of enlarging the existing engines without destroying their basic layout, and without incurring enormously high capital tooling costs. Not only the position of the cylinder centres, but the machined depth between top and bottom cylinder block faces also had to be preserved.

As the cylinder walls of both engines already featured a great deal of siamezing—in other words, there was no water between adjacent pairs of cylinders—any further bore increase was out of the question. The only solution, therefore, (and one bound to be dubbed unfashionable according to the tenets of the period) was to increase the crankshaft throws, and therefore the stroke. This was something not so far done on the existing engines, and it is a credit to Triumph's improvising capabilities that it was actually achieved without a change to the depth of the cylinder blocks, and that the original connecting rods were retained.

For the six-cylinder engine, an increase in capacity from 1998 cc to 2498 cc was achieved by increasing the crank throw by 9.5 mm, and the stroke by 19 mm, which made the new dimensions a bore and stroke of 74.7 × 95 mm. This size was first revealed in the autumn of 1967, for the TR5 and TR250 sports cars, and it involved changes to the shape and 'barrelling' of the crankcase.

A similar increase in stroke for the four-cylinder engine would have brought the capacity up to 1621 cc, which was even more than was thought likely to be needed. Instead, a 1.5-litre limit was sought, and was achieved by a 5.75 mm increase in crank throw, or 11.5 mm increase in stroke, which meant that the new dimensions were 73.7 × 87.5 mm, and that the exact capacity was 1493 cc. Only minor changes were needed to the cylinder block, and none to the head, while the same connecting rods were retained.

The unit was first built into South African sourced Triumph models before the end of the 1960s, but its first British-built application was the front-wheel-drive Triumph 1500 saloon of August 1970. As far as the Spitfire was concerned, a prototype unit (with unspecified power output) was performance tested at MIRA in February 1966 when, with a 3.89:1 final drive ratio and 145-section radial ply tyres, the car achieved 95.5 mph, and a 0–60 mph acceleration time of 12.45 seconds. Note that this was a full year even before the normal 1147 cc engine was up-graded to 1296 cc in production-line Spitfires.

The 1493 cc Spitfire tune, therefore, was on its way to being settled well before the end of the 1960s and one important aspect of that early test was to prove that the ageing SC engine could produce very much the same performance in a Spitfire as could the PE150 slant-4 engine, without the need to spend any new capital on re-tooling the chassis frame and bonnet panels.

There was no rush, however, to bring the 1493 cc engine into production for the 1.3-litre engined car was still selling well, and was completely competitive with the Spridget. In addition, it was known that the BMC product had already reached the absolute limit of its engine, at 1275 cc. As Harry Webster said, when I talked to him about the life of the engine, 'Both the engines started out with exactly the same capacity of 803 cc and exactly the same bore and stroke, in the early 1950s, but we managed to get more than 200 cc extra out of our engine, and it could even have been a bit bigger if necessary. I've always been proud of that.'

With hoods erect, Spitfire 1500s looked much smarter than their pre-1970 counterparts had done

By the early 1970s, however, the need became urgent, at least for Spitfires to be sold in North America. In 1972 the 1296 cc engine became so strangled by the exhaust emission laws that it could only use a single Zenith-Stromberg carburettor, an 8.0:1 compression ratio, and it produced a mere 48 bhp (net) at 5500 rpm. This made the 1972-model car the least powerful of all Spitfires ever built, and pushed the maximum speed down towards 80 mph. The fact that BMC were also in trouble with their MG Midget and its 1275 cc engine was no consolation. Something had to be done.

The existing engine could not be made to breathe more deeply, for the 8.0:1 compression ratio was the maximum possible to allow the engine to run satisfactorily on the new-fangled low-octane unleaded petrol, and any changes to the camshaft lift or overlap made the question of exhaust gas mixture compliance more difficult to answer. Not only that, but in 1973 the regulations were scheduled to be more severe than in 1972.

The only answer was to enlarge the engine, from 1296 cc to 1493 cc, as already done for the Triumph 1500 saloon. Functionally, and practically, this was very easy to do, and there was virtually no external

difference between the two units, which shared the same basic block, head, and manifold castings, but the full programme of compliance tests had to be completed before it could go on sale. The most severe of these was that a 50,000-mile road test, under controlled conditions, had to be completed. Triumph carried out all such tests on the public road, on a closed circuit centred on Coventry. It needs little calculation to discover that, even when the car was being driven on a day-and-night basis, the 50,000 mile test could take up to six months to be completed. John Lloyd confesses that he used to have recurring nightmares about the possibility of such a test car being damaged in an accident when well on its way towards the end of the endurance runs; once, he recalls, it actually happened when one endurance car ran into the back of the other! Fortunately, the US authorities allowed an untouched engine to be transferred to another car for the job to be finished off.

For the United States *only*, therefore, the Mk IV gave way to the 1500 from the start-up of 1973 model-year, with a power boost from 48 bhp to 57 bhp, at a speed reduced from 5500 to 5000 rpm. More important, perhaps, with traffic driving in mind, was a boost in peak torque from 61 lb. ft at

BOTTOM: *Spitfire 1500s had polished wood fascia panels, but the style was still the same as that introduced at the end of the 1960s. This particular car is fitted with overdrive—the switch for which is in the gear-lever knob*

BELOW: *One detail of the Spitfire 1500 was the use of printed, rather than moulded badges to keep the public interested*

74 lb. ft at 3000 rpm. All this, incidentally, was achieved with the same single Zenith-Stromberg carburettor, and with the compression ratio reduced even more, to 7.5:1.

It worked, and the customers seemed to be happy. They were, in all probability, so shell-shocked by the way in which the new laws were tending to make all sports cars less sporting, slower, and heavier, that they were delighted to see Spitfire performance back up to a 94 mph top speed, even if it accelerated no better than the Mk 2 had done in 1965. There were, in any case, all the cosmetic changes detailed in Chapter 6 to be admired as well.

Road & Track did the Spitfire 1500 the honour of being a major road test feature in their New York International Automobile Show issue of May 1973,

when they raved so much about the fine handling that they said, 'It's now in the same league as the Datsun 240Z, the Fiat 124 Spider and the Lotus Elan Sprint!'. Praise indeed. Their car had the optional ($175) removable hardtop fitted, and they summed up the 1500 as: 'a reasonably modern, handsomely styled, decent performing and good handling open roadster. Of the cars in its class the Spitfire is probably the best.' The customers certainly seemed to agree. Even in 1972, when the gutless 48 bhp 1296 cc engine had been specified, it had outsold the Midget. In 1973, worldwide, 1701 more people bought Spitfires than Midgets.

1974 was like 1973, except that radial tyres were standardised for all markets including North America, and the axle ratio was back to 3.89:1. For 1975, after two years of widely-different specifications between markets, some sort of order was restored, when the 1296 cc Spitfire was finally laid to rest, the Mk IV died off, and all markets began to be supplied with the 1500 instead.

In Britain, however, the Spitfire 1500 was upstaged by the MG Midget 1500 for the first few weeks. As recounted in more detail in a later chapter, British Leyland rationalized their engine/

RIGHT: *For 1977, Spitfire 1500s were jazzed up with a new seat trim style, but no mechanical changes*

BELOW: *Spitfire 1500 engine installation, UK variety, virtually the same as the Mk IV which preceded it. Note the arrival of 'Rover-Triumph' identification*

sports car line-up from the end of 1974 by marrying the Spitfire 1500's engine to the MG Midget body and chassis; this derivative was displayed at the 1974 Earls Court Show, when an unmodified Spitfire Mk IV was on the Triumph stand. The European-specification Spitfire 1500 was actually unveiled at the Turin Show in November 1974, but the British press were not allowed to describe the car until the beginning of December. Another prime example of muddled British Leyland thinking.

There were no surprises. Visually, the under-bonnet installation of the 1493 cc engine looked just like that of the 1296 cc unit, even down to the same air cleaner box and flexible pipes leading forward to cold air inlets ahead of the radiator. Power was up from the 61 bhp (DIN) of the Mk IV, which had been slightly de-rated in 1972, to a very lusty 71 bhp (DIN) at 5500 rpm, and the torque shot up from 68 lb. ft at 2900 rpm to 82 lb. ft at 3000 rpm.

Hidden away was a gearbox change made in the

interests of rationalization. This will need a bit of careful explanation. In the beginning there was the Herald/Spitfire box, and this evolved into the all-synchromesh Spitfire/Vitesse/GT6 box. When Harry Webster came to move to Austin-Morris at Longbridge in 1968, and directed the evolution of the mass-market Morris Marina saloon, that new car's all-synchromesh gearbox was a further development of the Triumph GT6 unit, but re-developed to include a more compact single-rail selector change, and manufactured at Longbridge. Now, for the Spitfire 1500, the single-rail 'Longbridge/Marina' gearbox casing and single-rail change was adopted, but with the same set of internal ratios as the superseded Mk IV. Overdrive, as ever, was an optional fitting, and operated on top and third gears. To mark the lustier power output of the twin-SU 1493 cc engine, the final drive ratio was raised to 3.63:1 incorporating a ring and pinion set also built for the Morris Marina and for the Triumph Dolomite saloon.

Styling changes were confined to the use of 'Spitfire 1500' transfers applied to the nearside front of the bonnet panel and the boot lid, while at first there was a £39.78 'option pack' which included an

---

The neat front end of the Spitfire 1500, complete with under-bumper spoiler, print-on badging, and the latest under-riders

outside door mirror, a swivelling map reading lamp on the passenger's side of the fascia, a centre armrest, and head restraints to the top of the seats.

For the USA-market Spitfire 1500s, there was a 57 bhp engine as before, with a single Zenith-Stromberg CD4 carburettor, along with an air pump for the exhaust system, and exhaust gas recirculating valve to keep the emissions down. For California only, where the regulations were even more strict, a catalytic converter was added to the exhaust system for the first time.

As far as the British customer was concerned, the Spitfire 1500 was a reformed car. *Autocar*'s road test of March 1975 told it all, for they pinpointed a genuine two-way 100 mph maximum speed (the only time in which they cracked the three-figure barrier in a Spitfire) and they suggested that a typical day-in/day-out fuel consumption figure would be 32 mpg. Acceleration was sharper, in spite of the higher gearing, with 0–60 mph in 13.2 seconds, and the standing quarter-mile reached in 19.1 seconds.

As far as the British were concerned, the Spitfire carried on in production, more or less unchanged, until the summer of 1980, with no more mechanical

attention than that needed to keep it abreast of changing legislative requirements. Like the MG Midget, with which it now shared an engine, it seemed to be a forgotten car as far as British Leyland was concerned, for most sports car attention was being directed at the new TR7, its convertible and V8-engined developments, and the long-wheelbase derivative which was scheduled to follow.

Apart from the adoption of new seats and seat trims in the spring of 1977, along with TR7-type steering column electric switchgear, and a re-positioned steering lock/ignition key, the biggest news of the 1500's declining years were that it got 5.0 in. rim width wheels from the autumn of 1978. *Car* magazine, who could never be relied upon to give an old model an even break, began to caption its Spitfire summaries 'Death, where is thy sting', though, in fairness, they were also equally as rude about the MG Midget.

By 1975, and to meet USA safety regulations, Spitfire 1500s were kitted out with massive overriders, and had a built-in licence plate holder

I have deliberately stopped mentioning prices for the late-model Spitfires, simply because Britain was in the grip of serious inflation throughout the 1970s, and prices rocketed almost as fast as the new brochures advertising them could be printed. Purely for guidance, therefore, I will note that the re-styled Mk IV of late 1970 started life at £735 (basic), and that the price asked of the 1500 model when it went out of production in 1980 was £3631. Like that of any other British car, the price of a Spitfire had inflated by nearly 500 per cent in less than ten years.

Nevertheless, in Britain and in world-wide terms, the Spitfire continued to out-sell the Midget, and to justify its existence. Not even the Midget's engine transplant with a Triumph unit (a process which

caused apoplexy among some hide-bound MG enthusiasts) could tilt the balance, and the Midget was finally dropped at the end of the summer of 1979. Following the launch of the 1500 in Britain, sales perked up, to 4145 cars in 1978, but after that its popularity was on the slide. Only 935 were sold here in 1979, and 1164 in 1980.

Up until the end of the 1970s, however, the sales story in North America was more encouraging, even though little was done to the car other than to 'keep it legal'. Gradually but inexorably the car's weight crept upwards from about 1710 lb. in 1974 to 1875 lb. by 1980, to accomodate details like protective beams in the doors, and (from 1979) the use of energy-absorbing bumpers at front and rear.

From 1976, power outputs were officially no longer quoted. For one year only (1976), it was possible to get the compression ratio back up to 9.0:1 (except for California) which was the British/European level, but from 1977 it was down to 7.5:1 again, and a catalytic converter was specified for all

The last Spitfire of all, a UK-market model, rolling off the Canley production lines in August 1980. The hand-written placard on the nose reads, 'There she Blows'

models. In the car's last year of production, 1980, the exhaust emission regulations for California were so severe that the Spitfire was no longer sold there.

Even by the mid-1970s it was becoming clear that there would never be a replacement for the Spitfire. In the heady days of 1968–9, when the British Leyland corporation actually looked like making sense in the future (happy days. . .), it was widely rumoured that during the 1970s there *would* eventually be a new small sports car to take the place of the 'Spridgfire' models. It now appears that no serious work was ever carried out on such a project, and both Harry Webster and John Lloyd state quite definitely that Triumph never even started to design such a car; nor, as far as I know, did MG designers at Abingdon.

The Spitfire might, indeed, have found another home for final assembly towards the end of the 1970s if Leyland Cars (the names changed almost as often as the chairmen. . .) had managed to carry out their master plan for Rover-Triumph. Under that plan, the Canley assembly lines were to be closed and converted into a massive engine and transmission production factory for the rest of the group, and surviving Triumph models were to have been assembled at the vast new Rover assembly hall at Solihull.

That plan evaporated in the serious financial crisis of 1977–8, so much so that TR7 assembly was moved south from Liverpool to Canley, and Spitfire production stayed put. During 1980, however, TR7 assembly was progressively moved to Solihull, as it became clear that Spitfire and Dolomite production would merely be allowed to soldier on at Canley until they finally died away. Company documents I have seen suggested that the Spitfire would be built until 1982, but the change in the £/$ parity altered all that. As the £ rocketed in value to be worth more than $2.20 early in 1980, it made the sale of Spitfires in the United States no longer viable, and the last Spitfire of all was built at Canley in August 1980. No fewer than 314,342 Spitfires had been built in less than 18 years, of which 71,424 were originally delivered to British customers. As an export currency earner, the Spitfire was a phenomenal success, for 242,918 cars, 77.28 per cent of the total, had been sold overseas. The car's original 'mid-wives'—Harry Webster, George Turnbull, and Giovanni Michelotti—could be proud of themselves.

Facts and figures: Spitfire 1500

Built	December 1974 to August 1980
Number built	95,829
Chassis numbers	FH75001 onwards
	FM28001U onwards (USA)
	FM28001UC onwards
	(California)

Basic prices UK £1290 on announcement, rising to £3631 at August 1980 when discontinued (and still £3631 in Autumn 1981, as stocks ran out)

USA $3745 in 1975, rising to $5995 in 1980, and $6250 in 1981 for old stock

Engine 4-cyl, in-line, cast-iron cylinder block and cylinder head, three crankshaft main bearings. Bore, stroke and capacity 73.7 × 87.5 mm., 1493 cc (2.90 × 3.44 in., 91.1 cu. in.). CR 9.0:1, 2 SU carburettors. 71 bhp (DIN) at 5500 rpm. Maximum torque 82 lb. ft at 3000 rpm.

Transmission Final drive ratio 3.63:1. Overall gear ratios 3.63 (2.90 in optional overdrive top), 5.05, 7.84, 12.70, reverse 13.99:1. 18.0 mph/1000 rpm in direct top gear; 22.6 mph/1000 rpm in overdrive top gear.

Suspension and brakes 9.0 in. front disc brakes, 7 × 1.25 in. rear drums. 155-13 in. radial ply tyres on 4.5 in. rim bolt-on steel disc wheels.

Dimensions Length 12 ft 5 in.; width 4 ft 10.5 in.; height 3 ft 11.5 in. Front track 4 ft 1 in.; rear track 4 ft 2 in. Unladen weight (basic specification) 1750 lb.

Chapter 10
North American racer: always a winner

On the dashboard of every Spitfire since the mid-1970s, British Leyland/USA affixed a prominent brass plaque reading, 'SCCA [Sports Car Club of America] National Champion,' and listing the years to date that Spitfires had triumphed in America's most popular form of motor racing. The plaque, showing wins in 1965 and 1968 forward, is both an overstatement and an understatement. In 1971 and 1972, for example, the current Mk 3 1.3-litre Spitfire was beaten by Spridgets; it was the out-of-production 1147 cc Spitfire which carried the colours in those years, in a lower class—G-Production. On the other hand there were two years—1968 and 1975—when Spitfires were victorious in *both* the F- and G-Production classes. Overall, there was hardly a year between 1968 and 1980 when Spitfires failed to capture at least one championship.

The reasons for this long string of successes are several: a competitive basic specification; very strong factory support with a host of SCCA-legal competition options; and considerable financial backing from Standard-Triumph and later BL in the United States.

The campaign to make the Spitfire a winner began almost immediately following US introduction in 1963. The legendary 'Kas' Kastner, Standard-Triumph's phenomenally talented US competition manager, wrote a race-preparation booklet which the company flogged at $1.25 to anyone who expressed the slightest interest. The Kastner approach was not overly complex, but mainly a recitation of familiar razor-edge tuning techniques and certain Stanpart goodies. By similar methods, Kas had already created champion TRs.

By early 1964, the Spitfire parts list had grown considerably, and it's worth setting down, for it demonstrates the overkill of factory support and the remarkably low cost of race-prepping a Spitfire.

Number	Item	Price
V170	rear suspension camber compensator	$24.95
V172	competition four-branch exhaust system	67.00
V174	non-slip differential, 4.55:1 ratio	115.00
V175	'B' camshaft (for use with comp. valve springs	58.75
V176	competition valve springs	7.80
V177	oil radiator kit	69.95
V178	wide base (4½ in. rim) wheels, ea.	20.70
V181	Bendix electric fuel pump	25.75
V339	alternate (improved flow) grille assembly	29.95
V340	Koni competition front shock absorbers, ea.	24.00
V341	Koni competition back shock absorbers, ea.	24.00
V391	non-slip differential, 4.11:1 ratio	115.00
V392	non-slip differential (case only), 4.55:1	20.00
V393	non-slip differential (case only), 4.11:1	20.00
V398	competition rear brake linings, set	38.00
V399	competition front springs	15.50
V400	competition rear springs	40.00
V401	close-ratio transmission gear set	185.00
301698	differential cage unit	15.62
502017	4.87:1 rear axle ratio	27.87
502018	4.55:1 rear axle ratio	27.87
508904	complete nose section (4.87:1 gear ratio)	142.50
508905	complete nose section (4.55:1 gear ratio)	142.50
511401	overdrive kit	287.50
512339	competition front disc pads, set	12.88

Triumph's USA competitions supremo in the 1960s, who did so much to make the Spitfires and GT6s competitive, was Kas Kastner. This shot, in fact, shows him tickling up the Weber-carburetted engine of a 1964 works TR4

All of the above items were SCCA-approved for the Spitfire. The wide choice of axle ratios, Kastner pointed out, gave the driver flexibility to handle SCCA's variety of courses—from Riverside, California's long straights and high-speed corners to Thompson, Connecticut's twisty blacktop with its formidable up-hill-downhill hairpin. With the exception of non-slip differentials, close-ratio gearing and overdrive, a racing Spitfire could be built from these bits, none priced over $100 each. The racing camshaft alone brought bhp up to 70; Kastner called that Stage I. Stage II and III kits included a special (factory) four-port cylinder head yielding 80 and 90 bhp respectively. Stage III

included special rods, pistons and crank, and was expensive—$550 plus freight and duty.

It wasn't very long before racing Spitfires began to compete. A forecast of the future occurred in late 1965, at the American Road Race of Champions in Riverside, California. Held at the end of each season, the ARRC pits top drivers in each SCCA class from all geographical divisions, a monumental all-star show featuring the best cars from coast to coast.

The ARRC G-Production race was won convincingly that day by Ed Barker, his potent Spitfire prepared by him and his son Jerry. Ed was leading his class by lap three, after which he simply ran away and hid. His average speed was 0.7 mph faster than that of the F-Production winner! Underlining the Spitfire's potential, similar models driven by Dr Dave Kiser, Bob Clemens and Irwin Lorincz romped home 3-4-5, giving Triumph four of the five top positions.

In 1965, the SCCA decided to break down its competition and to award national championships to the top drivers in each of its six national divisions. By this time there was no dearth of Spitfires in SCCA class G-Production, previously the domain

RIGHT: *Works team line up, Sebring 1965. All four Le Mans Spitfires made the trip, but ADU3B was only used for practice. Peter Bolton rolled ADU1B during the race, and heavy repairs were needed before Le Mans in June*

BELOW: *Sebring 1965, and Peter Bolton's works Spitfire battles with one of the MG Midgets from Abingdon. Which looks more standard?*

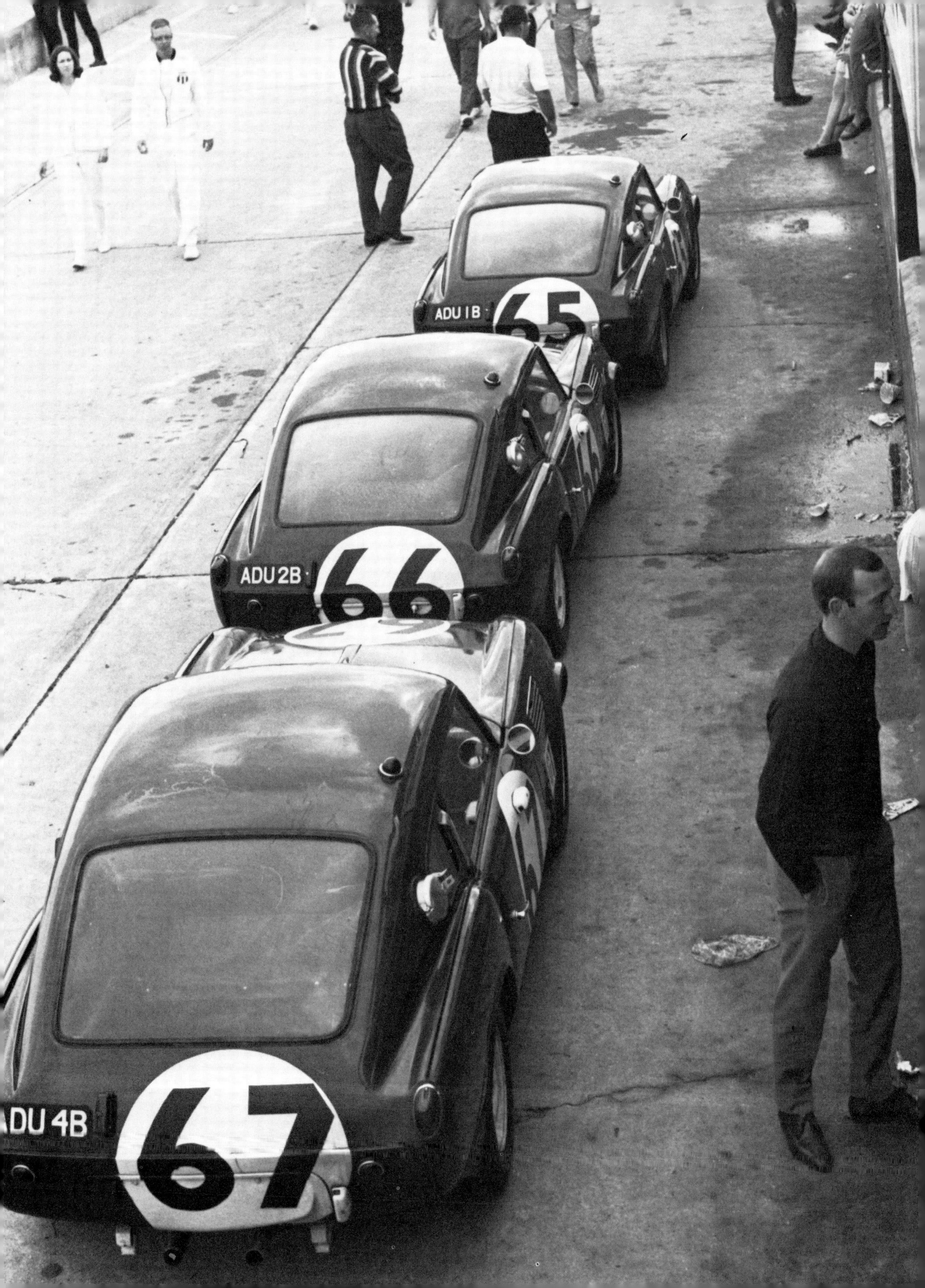
ADU 1B
65
ADU 2B
66
ADU 4B
67

of the 1.1-litre Spridget. One of the hottest drivers was Duane Feuerhelm of the Auto Works in Granada Hills, California, his Spitfire distinguished by Royal Air Force roundels on its rear wings. Duane's sequence began on 8 June at Laguna Seca, where he finished first overall, ahead of every G- and H-Production car, and the H-Modifieds as well. On 23 June at Riverside, he beat the Western Regional points leader Bill Young (Midget), finishing fourth in a G-Production/H-Modified contest. Again at Salt Lake City in a 7 July Divisional race, Feuerhelm beat Young in G-P and finished sixth in a field including the more rapid F-Production machinery.

Feuerhelm did less well in the rest of the season, and the Pacific Region championship fell to a Sprite. But meanwhile his compatriots in other areas

had been waging a Spitfire battle-royal, and when the smoke cleared the Midwest, Southeast and Southwest Regions had fallen to Triumph; Spitfires had won half of the six SCCA 1965 G-Production Championships.

In 1966–7, the Spitfire's dominance was broken temporarily by the new 1275 cc Sprites and Midgets, although there were moments of glory. Virginian Tony Adamowicz, for example, defeated a field including previously unbeaten Bill Koch (1275 Midget) in G-Production at the Grattan, Michigan SCCA nationals—and lowered the track record by three seconds. The great skein of success had to wait, though, until the 1296 cc Mark 3 arrived in America for the 1968 model year. From that point on, the Spitfire was virtually unbeatable.

The 1968 championship was won by Brian Fuerstenau a first-rate mechanic as well as a superb driver, backed by the legendary Group 44 team of Bob Tullius. With strong support from BL and Quaker State Oil, Group 44 has been the most successful Triumph racing team over the years, commencing with Bob Tullius's great 1962–4 performances in the TR4. Group 44 has raced every

Pre-Sebring scrutineering—someone obviously doesn't believe the legality of those splendid little cars. Leaning on the car is Ray Henderson, while Kas Kastner is in dark glasses

Triumph sports car, and is still winning with TR7s, TR8s and the Jaguar XJ-S. Fuerstenau romped home an easy victor in 1968, and Spitfires triumphed again in 1969 (Lee Mueller) and 1970 (John Kelly).

During 1971–2, the current Mark IV Spitfires were denied the F-P title by a fresh onslaught of Spridgets, but Mark 1 and 2 cars kept the flag flying with national championships in both years. The 1972 G-Production winner, Rick Cline, repeated his performance in 1973. (Followers of that inspiring act of civil disobedience, Brock Yates' 'Cannonball Baker Sea to Shining Sea Memorial Trophy Dash', will remember that Rick Cline holds the US coast-to-coast record, having travelled from New York to Los Angeles in 36 hours, driving a Ferrari Dino during the 1975 Cannonball.)

As the Spitfire began its long SCCA racing career in 1965, Kastner began to look for other ways to prove its prowess. He found one at Sebring, the great 12-hour Florida endurance race. Three lightweight works Spitfires with special coupé bodies—the 1964 Le Mans veterans, ADU1B/2B/4B—turned up to contest the 1965 GT category.

They were basically in their Le Mans state, as described elsewhere in these pages, but were given careful preparation by Kastner.

Alec Ullmann, president of the Automobile Racing Club of Florida and Sebring's leading official, remembers 1965 for two reasons, 'First, it brought about the quite unexpected win of an American-built car (the Chaparral), made in Texas and equipped with an automatic transmission which, by all the traditions of the game, was totally and strictly impossible. Second, it was run part of the time under a deluge that, I am sure, set a record in precipitation at any time, anywhere!' (The rest of the time it was broiling hot—track temperature got up to 130 degrees during the afternoon.)

Finishing order in the 1968 American Road Race of the Champions—with Brian Fuerstenau winning in the Group 44 Mk 3, from Lee Meuller in the Triumph Competitions (Kastner-West Coast) entry. Fuerstenau won SCCA F-Production outright in 1968

The three fastback Spitfires—they looked much like the forthcoming GT6, except for aerodynamic front ends with faired-in, covered headlamps—were competing mainly against similar-displacement GT class cars like the Spridgets and smaller Alfas. All three roared off in unison from the Le Mans start but Peter Bolton rolled ADU1B in the first half hour and retired. The other two cars, with racing numbers 66 (Tullius/Gates) and 67 (Barker/Feurhelm/Rothschild), just kept reeling off laps. Directed by team manager Kastner, they averaged about four minutes per circuit, close to 80 mph. Towards twilight—the worst possible time—came the downpour. Ullmann remembers cars like the Spitfires roaring past the big-block monsters who were struggling to maintain any grip on the track surface. Noted that *Triumph Newsletter, (USA)* '... it was just so darned amusing to see the GT Spitfires hydroplaning past Ferraris, Ford GTs, Cobras ... and the Chaparral.'

Slagle leads Meuller, Road Atlanta, 1972—typical of close Spitfire racing in SCCA F-Production events

Only 40 of the 69 starters were still alive at the 12th hour, and two of them were Spitfires. They finished 29th and 30th overall, second and third in class. Duane Feurhelm in ADU4B was first to finish, having completed 163 laps, just 46.8 miles less than the works TR4. 'The cars ran beautifully,' continued the *Newsletter*—'in the heat, and in the rain: the standard of driving of the Triumph team was of the highest order. Kastner was like Kastner—which means he did a great job as team manager. Ray Henderson and his crew of mechanics from the factory in England were just fantastic—tireless, enthusiastic and skilled. So much effort goes into a project of this nature, and there are always unsung heroes. Without people like this, Triumph at Sebring '65 would not have happened.'

Kas Kastner retired as Triumph competitions manager in 1970, establishing Kastner-Brophy Inc. in Gardena, California. There, he built a body for a rocket-powered land speed record car and prepared a Lola for the SCCA Continental Championship. But Kas remained close to Triumph, and helped prepare the GT6 for SCCA competition after it arrived in the United States.

Although certain compromises had been made in its spec. for the sake of smoothness and ride comfort, the GT6 proved remarkably competitive. Assigned to SCCA class E-Production—a difficult category including Porsche 914s and MGBs—the GT6 campaigned with moderate success in 1967–8 and won the championship in 1969 and 1970. The winning drivers, respectively, were Mike Downs and Don Devendorf—the same Devendorf who'd brought Spitfire its second G-Production title in 1968. In fact, the GT6 performed so well in 1970 that SCCA bumped it up to D-Production in 1971, where it was plainly no match for the Datsuns and Jensen-Healeys. Nevertheless, a Kastner-Brophy GT6 Mark 3 with Devendorf up won two big races in February 1972, and came within 9 points of the Divisional D-Production championship. Dave Dooley and Rick Cline also won important 1972 D-P races, proving that the GT6 was still a car the competition could not overlook.

The small-engined Spitfire's last championship year was 1975, when young Jerry Barker campaigned in a Mark 2—the same model his father had raced with distinction ten years before. By then,

factory interests were mainly behind the current production models. Though 1971–2 did not see F-Production titles, the 1300s and 1500s achieved a death grip on that class in 1973. Through 1980, Spitfire was national F-P champion seven times, missing only in 1976.

Even the other years were full of interest. Going into the last month of the 1971 season, Spitfires had won 26 of 38 national F-P races, Group 44's John Kelly scoring a perfect six-win record (matched by teammate Brian Fuerstenau in a GT6). Good seasons were also enjoyed by Lee Mueller, Jim Ray, Ken Slagle, John Howard and Jim Speck. In addition to the F-P wins, 1147 cc Spitfires posted seven G-P victories and GT6s ten in D-P. The TR6, by contrast, held only four. Perhaps not by coincidence, Spitfire was Triumph's volume leader for 1971, when the marque as a whole recorded

---

John McComb was competitive in 1972 with the Quaker State/ British Leyland TR6. In 1973 he was less successful in the D-Production GT6. Super fast Datsun chases

21,000 US sales—second only to 1959's record 23,000.

Again in 1972, though Spitfire wasn't F-P champ, no one could gainsay its performance. Kastner-Brophy's chief engineer Doug Brown saw many successes with his 1300. By mid-July the Triumph had racked up the following SCCA scores:

	GT6 D-P	Spitfire F-P	G-P
1st	12	15	16
2nd	3	3	8
3rd	3	7	10

The 1972 record book was full of big Spitfire wins: Gary Oullett and Rick Cline in F- and G-Production at Road Atlanta; Slagle and Royer at Thompson; Kelly at Elkhart Lake; Bob Ballou in G-P at Laguna Seca. It was a very Triumphant

John Kelly, F-Production winner in 1970 and 1973 in Spitfires, speeds on to another victory. Note hefty roll-over bar and Minilite wheels

year. When Kelly won the F-Production title in 1973 and started Spitfire on its almost unbroken skein of championships, people almost became resigned to Spitfire's invincibility.

In assessing the car's North American racing history, Canadian performances must be noted. In 1965, the Canadian Auto Sports Club created a category called 'improved production.' This allowed Ray Gray of Whitby, Ontario, to build himself a Spitfire that would run with the vaunted Porsche 356 Carrera, and even come within striking distance of a Lotus 47!

The CASC rules allowed Gray to lighten and streamline his Spitfire, as well as modify its engine. He duly smoothed out the front end with headlamp covers, undershield and airscoop. Wheel arch extensions protected seven-inch American Racing mag wheels. Under the hood was Kastner's Stage 2 head, with Weber carbs on a special manifold—though remarkably, the pistons were stock and the cam was a normal Kastner grind. The suspension mods were taken right out of Kastner's book and the Stanpart bins.

Gray began competing with this very special

Spitfire in 1965: through 1967, he won the CASC class 6/7 championship every year. His record was awesome: 11 wins in his first 12 1966 races, 12 for his first 13 in 1967. Racing with 1600 cc class cars he usually finished third, right behind two Porsche Carreras. His time around Mosport was 2.4 seconds faster than Bob Tullius' own TR4.

Then there was that American phenomenon, the economy run—and Spitfires did well here too. In 1965, Auto Works in Granada Hills, California set up a Spitfire for the 13th Los Angeles to Las Vegas 291-mile economy run. They used a brand new Mark 2 Spitfire, with a special fastback to improve slip and the driver was sales manager Jack Draper. The Spitfire won its class and finished 7th overall, averaging 56.92 miles per gallon or 59.20 ton miles.

Nor must we forget The Great Spitfire Challenge Race at Road Atlanta in November, 1973. This was a match race between Bob Tullius and Canadian driver Stephanie Ruys de Perez, who had challenged the affable Bob at Bryar, New Hampshire the previous September. The cars were matched Spitfire 1500s, supplied by BL/USA, virtually stock, bearing *Venus* and *Mars* racing emblems. The five-lap contest saw an exciting dice with Tullius just pulling it out by 1.8 seconds. His reward was a magnificent silver-plated trophy crowned with a very realistic *Male Chauvinist Pig*. The award ceremony was spiced up when the starter was attacked by Women's Libbers for dropping the chequered flag too soon. The starter was doused with a bucket of water, but Tullius lived to race again in the TR6, and Stephanie returned to her Mini for the season of 1974.

There was just no end to competition variety for the Triumph Spitfire.

Triumph Spitfire Production Racing Championships
Sports Car Club of America

Year	G-Production (1147 cc cars)	F-Production (1296/1493 cc cars)
1965	Dave Kiser (Midwest)	
	Don Kearney (Southeast)	
	Don Smith (Southwest)	
1968	Don Devendorf	Brian Fuerstenau
1969		Lee Mueller
1970		John Kelly
1971	Marshall Meyer	
1972	Rick Cline	
1973	Rick Cline	John Kelly
1974		Rick Cline
1975	Jerry Barker	Ken Slagle (1500)
1976		
1977		Tom Collier (1500)
1978		Jack May (1500)
1979		Steve Johnson (1500)
1980		Jerry Barker (1500)
1981		
	6 in 15 seasons	10 in 14 seasons

Triumph GT6 Production Racing Championships

1969	Mike Downs (E-Production)
1970	Don Devendorf (E-Production)

Chapter 11
Spitfire dependents:
Happy 'extended' family

If you looked hard enough, and knew where to look, there was evidence of major components from the Spitfire being used in many other cars during the 1960s and 1970s. The variety, and scope, was enormous, for it ranged from the use of front suspension items in the Cooper and Brabham Grand Prix cars of the early 1960s, to complete engine transplants in the MG Midget of the 1970s. Indeed, the Spitfire, like several other great cars, found itself cast in the role of Universal Provider.

It is only fair, of course, to point out once again that much of the Spitfire's basic engineering came from that of the Herald, though for the Spitfire a lot of re-development, evolution, and beefing up took place. In addition, such was the cross-pollination of engineering between one Triumph car and another in the 1960s that it was often difficult to decide where a true 'parentage' lay.

The basic Spitfire/GT6 chassis frame and bodyshells were not 'loaned out' to any other significant manufacturer, which is only reasonable, as this would really have amounted to building under licence. The backbone frame, in fact, complete with most of the running gear, has been used under more than one 'kit car', most notable of which was the Spartan, an MG TF look-alike using modern components.

Once the Standard-Triumph engine had been enlarged from 948 cc to 1147 cc, and power-tuned for fitment to the Spitfire in 1962, it became attractive to specialist manufacturers who could not afford to develop their own units. The major competition, of course, always came from the BMC A-Series unit, which was superficially easier to tune further, and which was offered by BMC at an even more attractive price. Ultimately, therefore, it must have been humiliating for a former BMC company, MG at Abingdon, to have to accept a Spitfire engine as a major modification to the MG Midget.

By the early 1970s, the MG Midget was in trouble. It was a car which had almost wilfully been ignored by British Leyland since that corporation was founded in 1968. A successor to the Midget and MGB (EX234), designed at about the time of the Leyland-BMH merger, was cancelled, US-sourced emissions and safety legislation took up an increasing amount of time among the MG designers at Abingdon, and the Midget's design stagnated.

Exhaust emission legislation intensified as the 1970s progressed. The Midget's 1275 cc BMC A-Series engine, like that of the Spitfire, suffered severely in the process. Triumph, at least, could claw back some much-needed horsepower by enlarging the Spitfire's engine size from 1296 cc to 1493 cc, but MG could not. The A-Series had reached the practical limit of its capacity—1275 cc—in 1964, and nothing more could be done. Once BL's sports cars were integrated into a single selling organization in North America, based at Leonia, New Jersey, some sort of rationalization became desirable. The Spitfire became a 1500 in North America for the 1973 model-year, with great success. It was during 1973, therefore, that the decision was taken to transplant the Triumph engine into the Midget—a change to take effect late in 1974, for the 1975 model-year.

Getting the Spitfire engine into the engine bay of the Midget was surprisingly straightforward, not

---

ABOVE RIGHT: *More Triumph Herald based than Spitfire, perhaps—note the doors—the Bond Equipe attempted increased performance by reducing weight. A contemporary photograph from the Triumph Cars' archive!*

RIGHT: *MG TF lookalike but based on the Spitfire running gear. Once of the better 'kit cars' the RMB Gentry satisfies many customers*

withstanding the fact that all BMC A-Series engines had had their carburettors and exhaust manifolds on the left side of the engine bay (near the [British] kerb side), and that the Spitfire's carbs and manifolds were on the right. The Spitfire installation was, however, a little bulkier, and for use in the Midget a different exhaust manifold and air filters were needed.

British MG enthusiasts, predictably, howled their disgust that this should have been done, quoting the fact that *official* (as opposed to actual) peak power and torque figures were little changed. This strident reaction, of course, ignored the real reason for the change—that British Leyland wanted to rejuvenate North American sales of Midgets, which were much more numerous than those made in the rest of the world.

LEFT : *Many racing car chassis designs used the S-T wishbone and upright front suspension. Cooper started, Lotus continued (here on the Europa)*

BELOW : *Morgan 4/4 lookalike, the Burlington, really is superbly finished. Few would readily appreciate that the Spitfire chassis lurks beneath. With this quality building such cars satisfies both traditionalists and aesthetics*

In any case, there was another basic flaw in the protestors' argument—the Midget 1500 was substantially faster in acceleration and top speed than the obsolete 1275 cc Midget, and was at least as economical, and this was in spite of the extra weight of the '5 mph' bumpers which all Midgets had to lug around from this date. A Midget 1500 could beat 100 mph, and reach 60 mph in 12.3 seconds, which compared well with a 94 mph maximum speed, and 0–60 mph in more than 14 seconds for the A-Series 1275 cc car.

Thus equipped, the Triumph-engined Midget remained in production until the end of 1979 (final stocks not being cleared until mid-1981, in fact, in North America), and a total of 73,899 cars were built. Somehow or other, MG enthusiasts never had an answer for the fact that so many were sold. . . .

The Spitfire engine, brakes, and a few other minor components, also found their way into the Bond Equipe GT, which was a four-seater fastback coupé built in Preston, using the Herald's chassis and suspension, and being officially approved and distributed by chosen Triumph dealers. This car, and its descendant the Equipe GT 4S, remained in production until the end of the 1960s, when Bond were taken over (and speedily killed off) by Reliant.

More than one specialist manufacturer found the Spitfire's engine, and its chassis-mounted final-drive, very useful to them. TVR of Blackpool, for instance, offered a 1300 model for a short time, which featured a 1296 cc Spitfire engine, while their cars also used Spitfire/GT6 final-drive units on lower-powered derivatives of the basic multi-tubular chassis'd fibreglass bodied designs. Fairthorpe, who had various homes in the Home Counties in the 1960s and 1970s, gradually developed the Electron Minor on their own tubular frame, around the more and yet more powerful versions of the Spitfire's engine and gearbox.

Frankly, I am not at all surprised that the Herald/Spitfire swing axle rear suspension was not taken up by any of the specialist manufacturers, as it did not have desirable characteristics. On the other hand, it was eminently reasonable that the front suspension, or many of the components, should have been in great demand.

Harry Webster's engineers had produced a most remarkable coil spring independent front suspension for the Herald, and this was used, in strengthened and refined form, for the Spitfire and later the GT6 sporting cars. Not only did it have very satisfactory geometry, but it also had the most remarkable lock, and this made it attractive to other manufacturers who could not afford to develop their own assemblies. The particular attraction of the vertical link, or 'king post' as it would once have been known, was that it incorporated a ball joint at the top, a trunnion at the bottom, and the ability to be fitted inside a 13 in. wheel. In the face of less suitable components from Austin, Morris, Ford and Vauxhall, the Herald/Spitfire suspension soon found itself used in most remarkable places.

In particular, the vertical link was used by racing car manufacturers in their own front suspension. Perhaps it was John Cooper who first applied it to his single-seaters at the end of 1959—certainly by 1961 his Grand Prix cars also used it, and this undoubtedly influenced Jack Brabham to enact the same trick when he went off to found his own company in 1962. When Colin Chapman turned to building mid-engined cars for 1960, he also took up with the Spitfire's front suspension vertical link, but abandoned it for the Lotus 24 and 25 Grand Prix cars of 1962.

The Spitfire 1500 engine shoe-horned into the MG Midget. With the A series too tired for the North American market the 1500 was readily available

As Grand Prix cars became progressively more specialized, and needed much wider wheel rims, constructors had to design their own light-alloy vertical links, and by the mid-1960s the use of this Triumph item was confined only to smaller single-seaters. The advent of Formula Ford, however, gave it a whole new lease of life, for such low-cost racing cars benefitted enormously from the availability of such a versatile item.

Lotus used the vertical link and the top wishbones as part of the front suspension of their exciting Elan sports car, announced within days of the Spitfire itself, though they tried to wrap up the identity of the parts by referring to the use of a 'standard Alford and Alder wheel post'; Alford and Alder, of course, were specialist suppliers of steering and suspension components, but were also a wholly owned subsidiary of Standard-Triumph.

When the mid-engined Europa of 1967 was announced, this too had most of the Spitfire's front suspension, along with the same Girling disc brake and caliper installation, and (like the Elan) the rack and pinion steering. When many of the same items were to be found in the long-wheelbase Lotus Elan Plus 2 of 1967, the 'set' was complete. It was not until the new generation of Lotus models were introduced, in 1974 and 1975, that the BL/Alford and Alder connection was lost.

The 1974 MG Midget with 1500 Triumph Spitfire engine and gearbox. A sad conclusion for many MG fans

Appendix 1   Spitfire/Spridget—winners and losers: cars built per calendar year

Year	Spitfire	Spridget total	—of which	
			Sprite	*Midget*
1958		8729	8729	
1959		21566	21566	
1960		18665	18665	
1961		17715	10059	7656
1962	1355	21947	12041	9906
1963	20950	16477	8852	7625
1964	23387	22607	11157	11450
1965	19966	18044	8882	9162
1966	17077	13866	7024	6842
1967	15235	15225	6895	8330
1968	19599	14421	7049	7372
1969	18574	19214*	6129	13085
1970	17041	16103	1292	14811
1971	20577	17432	1022	16410
1972	19756	16158		16158
1973	15689	14130		14130
1974	13999	12449		12449
1975	15591	14502		14502
1976	18909	17121		17121
1977	17716	14340		14340
1978	21189	15400		15400
1979	10276	9777		9777
1980	7456			
Total	314342	355888	129362	226526

*1969 was the *only* year in which the *Spridget* outsold the Spitfire

Appendix 2   Spitfire production—1962 to 1980

Year	Home market	Export market	Percentage exports	Yearly total
1962	457	880	64.9	1355
1963	3685	17265	82.4	20950
1964	4965	18422	78.8	23387
1965	4327	15639	78.3	19966
1966	4416	12661	74.1	17077
1967	5420	9815	64.4	15235
1968	4563	15036	76.7	19599
1969	3704	14870	80.1	18574
1970	4534	12507	73.4	17041
1971	5328	15249	74.1	20577
1972	7077	12679	64.2	19756
1973	4082	11607	74.0	15689
1974	2743	11256	80.4	13999
1975	2627	12964	83.2	15591
1976	4117	14792	78.2	18909
1977	3117	14599	82.4	17716
1978	4145	17044	80.4	21189
1979	935	9341	90.9	10276
1980	1164	6292	84.4	7456
Totals	71424	242918	77.3	314342

| **Model totals** | Mk 1 45763 | Mk 2 37409 | Mk 3 65320 | Mk IV 70021 | 1500 95829 |

Even though the last Spitfire was built in 1980, by which time the GT6 had been obsolete for seven years, they have not become forgotten cars. Parts will still be available from BL's Unipart division for a number of years, and there is growing enthusiasm for the cars among specialist clubs.

This sort of thing seems to happen to so many cars. Owners, factory, and specialist press were all interested in developments when the models were relatively new. In the mid-1970s, however, when the Spitfire had to soldier along, on its own, it retreated into the shadows. Now that you can no longer buy a new one from Triumph showrooms, demand for good 'classic' examples, and for the expertise needed to rebuild down-at-heel models, is increasing rapidly.

Where are they now? Sales statistics make it clear that many of the surviving cars must be in North America, though I should make it clear that the Spitfire was more of a world-wide success story than, say, the MG, MGB or the Big Healey. Of 314,342 Spitfires and 40,926 GT6s built, 139,547 Spitfires and 22,658 GT6s were sold in the United States, very roughly speaking, about 50 per cent of production in each case.

On the other hand, 71,424 Spitfires (23 per cent), and a similar proportion of GT6s were sold in Britain, and the balance was spread very widely all round the world, the old 'Empire' countries like South Africa, Canada and Australasia taking a major share.

At the time of writing the original edition of this book (1982), there appears to be no serious difficulty in finding mechanical spare parts, and most of the important body panels are still available. In North America, the fact that the dealer network has contracted markedly in recent years does not help. Many ex-Triumph dealerships, however, still stock parts and service literature. If any Spitfire/GT6 owner out there needs help from US headquarters, he can find them at Leonia, New Jersey—and any existing Jaguar dealership will put him in touch with the appropriate specialist. My own grateful thanks in compiling this book go to Michael Cook, who is Public Relations Manager of Jaguar Rover Triumph Inc., who is not only a good professional, but has also written a neat little Spitfire handbook of his own, and is one of the few JRT men with an eye to the marque's heritage. You will find him at:

Jaguar Rover Triumph Inc.,
600 Willow Tree Road,
Leonia,
New Jersey 07605, USA   Tel: (201) 461-7300

In Britain, parts can be found through any Triumph dealer (and, at the last count, there were 950 of them), and the supply is co-ordinated from the Unipart operation at Cowley, near Oxford. Owners in other countries are advised to approach their concessionaires for major items which a small dealer may not stock.

Because the cars are built around strong, separate, box-section chassis frames, they have a much better chance of surviving their first 10 neglected years of life than a cheap monocoque car like an Austin-Healey Sprite/MG Midget. I have seen many Spitfires with very scruffy bodies, under which the frame is, if not as good as new, certainly very serviceable, and easily restored. The corrosion points are obvious, when they occur, and can be dealt with in a straightforward manner. Apart from the area under the half shafts, at the rear, where water tends to collect, the most obvious places to look are where the front suspension, steering, and rear suspension linkages connect to the frame. Fortunately, because the frame is so simple, and so accessible in most cases, you can repair, or reinforce, any trouble spots.

Linkages tend to go somewhat rattly with age, mainly because cheap bushes wear out, or become distorted. These are the items any specialist club tends to identify very early on. To an enthusiast I would say—think in terms of a really thorough 'chassis check-up' once a year, and don't hesitate to re-bush and re-shim as necessary; it will save more major expenditure in the long run. One noteworthy problem area, with old age, is where the rear suspension radius arms pick up to the bodyshell behind the seats. The body panels can given trouble, particularly if they have been thoroughly wetted from *both* sides (remember that open cars often get water in from above as well!).

Body panels are still available, in most cases, though Mk 1 and Mk 2 Spitfire bonnets ('low-bumper' layout) are now almost impossible to find. Indeed, any pre-1970 facelift panels are obviously in short supply, especially in countries where the volume of cars sold was rather limited. Bad rusting may eventually lead to inner wheel arch pressings in that bonnet assembly coming adrift, the same problem occurring at the rear, and in the body floors becoming very dog-eared. The stowage area, in particular, may have suffered badly, not only from water leaks, but from the way that items were often stowed loose in these cars, and might have chipped away at the paintwork inside.

Most panels on Spitfires and GT6s can be replaced, if not easily, at least in a conventional manner. If, however, a car has severe rusting on the body sills under the doors, this is more serious; not only does it result in substantial weakening of the structure, but it is much more costly to eradicate.

In general, the engines and transmissions are long-lasting and very simple to maintain. Be sure, however, that the oil pressure stays up to its designed level (40–60 psi), as bearings are quite narrow, and fairly highly stressed. The valve gear may be rattly, which is fairly normal, but the clearances should always be kept to the nominal rating. Gearboxes and back axles are a bit more vulnerable to neglect, and the early Spitfire components were not as strong as might have been desirable. Look very carefully for jumping out of reverse gear (expensive), and for 'clonk' and excessive clearance down the drive line, particularly in the final drive area (also potentially troublesome and expensive).

The major problem with older Spitfires, where originality is concerned, is that many soft trim items (carpet, seat, and door coverings, for example) are quite simply no longer stocked, and a number of cars have often been repaired with what we would now call 'unoriginal' items. The rubber mats from Mk 1 Spitfires, for example, wear fairly rapidly, and cannot now be replaced. The specialist clubs, however, as they grow larger, are trying to have such items re-manufactured.

Although there is usually a branch of a Triumph club in most countries, these tend to concentrate on the TR sports cars. In recent years, however, interest in the Herald/Vitesse/Spitfire/GT6 models has revived strongly, and the major club in this field is British, and is the Triumph Sports Six Club. At the time of writing, this club is expanding fast, so anyone interested should contact:

John Griffiths,
President, Triumph Sports Six Club,
55 The Churchills,
Highweek,
Newton Abbot,
Devon, UK

John will be interested in the formation of branches all over the world, and can put new members in touch with spares secretaries, technical specialists, and registrars for their particular model.

What model would I now buy? This is an almost impossible-to-answer question, for my preferences will certainly not be those of every Triumph enthusiast. However, here goes:

If I was buying a Spitfire, I feel that it would have to be one equipped with overdrive, wire wheels, and probably the optional hardtop (which I would take off as often as possible). Of all the derivatives, I always liked the Mk 3 (1967–1970 model), which was quicker than the Mk 4 which replaced it, and of all the 1500s the earlier examples built in 1975 and 1976 seemed to be the lightest and best built.

A choice of GT6s is somewhat easier. I am afraid I would not go out looking for a Mk 1, if it had the original rear suspension. Therefore, I would be looking for a Mk 2 and pre-1973 Mk 3, for these were the cars with the relatively advanced 'lower-wishbone' independent rear suspension. I would want my GT6 to have overdrive (most of them seemed to have it, in any case, and it *is* possible to update a GT6 or a Spitfire with an overdrive if you feel like tackling it), though as this was a heavier car I would not be as anxious to have wire wheels fitted. As an absolute preference, I would like to have a car with the restyled bodywork, for I admired the way Michelotti tidied up the original tail, and made the nose even smoother. Therefore, I plump for a 1970–1972 Mk 3, with overdrive, and as many of the extras as I can find fitted.

Index